Student Manual

Applying Career Development Theory to Counseling

FIFTH EDITION

Richard S. Sharf
University of Delaware

Prepared by

Richard S. Sharf
University of Delaware

BROOKS/COLE
CENGAGE Learning™

Australia • Brazil • Japan • Korea • Mexico • Singapore • Spain • United Kingdom • United States

ISBN-13: 978-0-495-80478-9
ISBN-10: 0-495-80478-9

Brooks/Cole
10 Davis Drive
Belmont, CA 94002-3098
USA

Cengage Learning is a leading provider of customized learning solutions with office locations around the globe, including Singapore, the United Kingdom, Australia, Mexico, Brazil, and Japan. Locate your local office at: **www.cengage.com/global**

Cengage Learning products are represented in Canada by Nelson Education, Ltd.

For your course and learning solutions, visit **www.cengage.com**

Purchase any of our products at your local college store or at our preferred online store **www.ichapters.com**

Printed in the United States of America
2 3 4 5 6 7 14 13 12 11

PREFACE

The purpose of the Student Manual is to assist students in learning the material described in Applying Career Development Theory to Counseling, Fifth Edition. The manual is divided into five sections for most of the 16 chapters that are in the textbook. I have tried to make this manual interesting and informative.

CHAPTER OUTLINE Each chapter starts with a one page overview of the chapter that includes the concepts that are important for each theory. You can use these pages to make notes as you prepare for exams. The outline follows the outline in the textbook.

EXERCISES These exercises are designed to apply the theory that is being described, to your own career development. The exercise should also help you understand the material in the chapter. It is probably best to do the exercise before you read the chapter. The exercises also can be used with individual and group career counseling in practica or in work settings. They are designed to help individuals understand their own career development.

CASE STUDIES Examples of applying career development theories to an individual should help you learn the concepts in the chapter. Multiple choice questions focus on concepts used in the case. Doing this section after reading the chapter should be helpful.

APPLYING CAREER DEVELOPMENT THEORY TO WOMEN AND CULTURALLY DIVERSE GROUPS Open-ended questions are designed to help you understand ways in which the theory can be applied to different groups of individuals.

STRENGTHS AND LIMITATIONS This section gives you an opportunity to state your views as to strengths and limitations of the theory.

QUIZZES At the end of each chapter are 10 true-false questions and 15 multiple choice questions that can help you prepare for exams. You may wish to use this section after reading the chapter or when you prepare for the exam. Answers to all true and false and multiple-choice questions are found at the end of each chapter.

SPECIAL NOTE Chapter 16 of the Student Manual includes multiple-choice questions that ask you to identify a theory that is associated with a specific concept or concepts.

Richard S. Sharf

TABLE OF CONTENTS

CHAPTER 1
INTRODUCTION

Definitions

    Career
    Job
    Occupations

The role of theory in psychology

General principles

    1. Explicit about rules and theorems
    2. Precise about limitations of
       predictions
    3. Need to be tested
    4. Need to be consistent and clear

Counselors use of career development theory

    Client population
    Theories of counseling and theories of
    career development
    Chunking

Counselor skills

    Helping skills

        Attending skills

        Questions

        Statements and reflections

        Continuation responses

        Giving information not opinion

        Family background exploration

        Assessment interpretation

Assessment instruments

    Definition of test

    Definition of inventory

    Norms

    Reliability

    Validity

Providing occupational information

How career development relates to career theory

Ethical principles

    Autonomy
    Nonmaleficence
    Beneficence
    Justice
    Fidelity

Career development of women

    Career development of culturally diverse
    populations

1

CHAPTER 1

INTRODUCTION

EXERCISE 1.1

REFLECTIONS ON WORK AND CAREER COUNSELING

E. 1a. What was the worst job that you have ever had?

_____

E. 1b. If you stayed at that job for 40 years, how would that affect your life?

_____

_____

_____

_____

E. 2. Think of someone you know who lost his or her job unexpectedly. What affect did that event have on that person?

_____

_____

_____

_____

E. 3a. Why did you go to college?

_____

_____

_____

E. 3b. What would your life be like if you did not go to college?

_____

_____

_____

2

E. 4. In what ways do you think career counseling skills are different from personal counseling skills?

_____

_____

_____

_____

E. 5. What do you think are appropriate goals for career counseling?

_____

_____

_____

_____

_____

IDENTIFYING AND USING BASIC CAREER COUNSELING SKILLS

Amy is a college freshman who has come to see you for career counseling at a college career center. Parts of the dialogue are presented in the questions below. For these questions you will be asked to choose the appropriate or best response to Amy.

1. Amy: "I thought I would be a psychology major when I came to college, but now I don't know what to do. It's not for me. I feel like I am falling behind other students who have picked a major."

    Choose the best counselor response from the choices below.

    a. You should think more carefully before changing from psychology.
    b. You sound really worried about what you might major in.
    c. What does your mother think you should major in?
    d. What were your grades in high school?

2. The best response to Question 1 is "b". This response would be called a(an)

    a. attending skill.
    b. content reflection.
    c. feeling reflection.
    d. giving information statement.

3. Amy replies to "You sound really worried about what you might major in," by saying: "I am finding that I really like biology. I was surprised. I am much more interested in it than I was in high school. Other students say biology is a major that takes too much work."

Choose the best counselor response from the choices below.

    a.   In what ways is college biology more interesting than high school biology?
    b.   Do you think the biology teacher you have had in college is better than the one you had in high school?

4. Identify the two types of question responses in Question 3.

    a.   (a) close-ended; (b) open-ended
    b.   (a) open-ended; (b) close-ended
    c.   (a) and (b) are close-ended
    d.   (a) and (b) are open-ended

5. Amy replies to the question: "In what ways is college biology more interesting than high school biology?" by saying: "I like the labs. They are more in depth than in high school. The teacher talks about processes like photosynthesis in lots of detail. I look forward to going to the labs. I think more about medicine as a possible career choice now."

Choose the best response to Amy's statement.

    a.   Do you think medicine is a good career for a woman?
    b.   Doesn't medicine require a great deal of work?
    c.   That's great that you are enjoying biology and the labs so much.
    d.   Psychology can be just as interesting as well.

6. The best response to Question 5 is "c". What type of response is "c"?

    a.   attending skill
    b.   giving information
    c.   giving opinion
    d.   reinforcement

7. Amy replies to "That's great that you are enjoying biology and the labs so much," by saying: "Yes. I like it a lot and am doing "A" work so far. Do you think that I will be able to get into medical school?"

Choose the best reply to Amy's question.

    a.   With A's in biology, you should have no problem getting into medical schools.
    b.   Medical schools in the U.S. often require an A- average or better. You can get more information from the Medical School Advisory Office.
    c.   I don't know.
    d.   If you keep your grades in all subjects at an A or A- level, you should not have a problem getting into medical school.

8. The answer to Question 7 is "b". The answer in response "b" is which type of response?

    a.   continuation response
    b.   giving information
    c.   giving opinion
    d.   test interpretation

9. Answers "a" and "d" in Question 7 would be identified as this type of response.

    a.   continuation response
    b.   giving information
    c.   giving opinion
    d.   test interpretation

EVALUATING AN ASSESSMENT INSTRUMENT

You have been asked to evaluate an assessment instrument. The questions below will give you some information and you will be asked to identify the measurement concept that is being discussed.

10. The instrument to be evaluated asks for opinions and has no right or wrong answers. It would be called a(an)

    a.   inventory.
    b.   test.

11. You are evaluating an inventory that measures work values. The instrument has been used at 12 different colleges. The inventory manual reports average scores for the males and females for each scale of the instrument. Also, there is information for each gender for freshmen, sophomores, juniors, and seniors. This information is referred to as

    a.   norms.
    b.   percentile scores.
    c.   reliability.
    d.   validity.

12. The inventory has been administered to 200 students on two occasions, 10 days apart. This sample of students scored very similarly on the instrument both times they took it. This is an indication of

    a.   high reliability.
    b.   low reliability.
    c.   high validity.
    d.   low validity.

13. This inventory has been found to be able to identify, to a reasonable degree, the major that students choose now. The concept being referred to is

    a.   construct validity.
    b.   concurrent validity.
    c.   predictive validity.
    d.   reliability.

14. The inventory has been shown to measure values that are similar to those measured by another values inventory. This information provides evidence that the instrument has

        a.   construct validity.
        b.   concurrent validity.
        c.   predictive validity.
        d.   reliability.

APPLYING CAREER DEVELOPMENT THEORY TO WOMEN AND CULTURALLY DIVERSE GROUPS

Why do you think career development theories may apply differently to men than to women?

_____

_____

_____

_____

_____

Why do you think that career development theories may apply differently to people from different cultures?

_____

_____

_____

_____

_____

INTRODUCTION TO APPLYING CAREER DEVELOPMENT THEORY TO COUNSELING: A QUIZ

True or false items: Decide if the following items are more "true" or more "false" as they apply to concepts discussed in this chapter.

T F Q1.   The counseling skills used in career counseling are similar to those used in personal counseling.

T F Q2.   If Gloria takes a job as a teller in a bank, that would be considered a part of her career.

T F Q3.   The work of a teller in any bank is considered an occupation.

T F Q4.   Theories of all types are abstract and do not need to be tested or researched.

T F Q5.   Theories need to be clear about their terms.

6

T F Q6. An example of an open-ended question is "Do you like this book?"

T F Q7. To say to a client, "Tell me more," is to use a continuation response.

T F Q8. Having a group of students take an interest inventory twice to see if their scores on the inventory scales will be consistent refers to a type of validity.

T F Q9. A code of ethics is very different for counselors doing career counseling than for those who do personal counseling.

T F Q10. One aspect of ethics for career counselors is that they should do no harm.

Multiple choice items: Select the best answer from the alternatives given.

Q11. Career counseling includes issues that

    a.   relate only to careers.
    b.   are not emotional.
    c.   may feel very personal to the client.
    d.   reveal a lack of time perspective.

Q12. If a position for an insurance agent is advertised in a magazine, that position can be considered a

    a.   career.
    b.   career theory.
    c.   job.
    d.   work task.

Q13. Monica changes from being an electrical engineer to studying dentistry. This statement refers to Monica's

    a.   career.
    b.   niche.
    c.   job.
    d.   occupation.

Q14. Which of these is most important in a good theory?

    a.   clarity
    b.   ethics
    c.   creativity
    d.   skillfulness

Q15. To test a theory, the theory should generate

    a.   adherents.
    b.   articles.
    c.   new career counseling techniques.
    d.   research.

Q16. Using the concept of *chunking*, counselors should be able to

    a.   group a limited number of theoretical concepts.
    b.   suggest many occupations for clients to consider.
    c.   use five or six inventories at a time with clients.
    d.   violate ethical rules without fear of punishment.

Q17. Maintaining good eye contact with a client is a good example of

    a.   attending skills.
    b.   continuation responses.
    c.   reflections.
    d.   reinforcement.

Q18. Which of the following is an example of giving information not opinion?

    a.   It's great that you did so well on the exam.
    b.   There are good examples of resumes in published books.
    c.   You seem to have what it takes to be a baseball coach.
    d.   You should listen to your father's advice about going on to college.

Q19. In constructing a test or inventory, a normative sample is used. Such a sample should

    a.   be individually selected by the researcher.
    b.   be typical of the population that is likely to use the inventory.
    c.   have mastered the subjects being assessed.
    d.   be responsible in their behavior and have no criminal record.

Q20. Dividing an assessment instrument and comparing each half to the other is a way of assessing

    a.   construct validity.
    b.   content validity.
    c.   split half reliability.
    d.   test retest reliability.

Q21. Comparing airplane mechanics' scores on a test of mechanical achievement to ratings of specific job performance would be an example of

    a.   content validity.
    b.   concurrent validity.
    c.   construct validity.
    d.   predictive validity.

Q22. Using assessment inventories in counseling can help clients make career decisions. Another use of inventories and tests is to

    a.   make career counseling more economical.
    b.   give the counselor outside help by using inventories.
    c.   provide useful occupational information.
    d.   develop and verify a theory.

Q23. The statement "I enjoy writing computer programs" is an example of

    a.   crosstalk.
    b.   psychtalk.
    c.   occtalk.
    d.   walktalk.

Q24. Which of the following is NOT a principle of ethical standards?

    a.   autonomy
    b.   consistency
    c.   justice
    d.   nonmalficence

Q25. Which of the following is NOT an accurate statement about ethics in career counseling?

    a.   Career theorists assume their theories will be used ethically.
    b.   Many counseling and helping professional organizations have very similar ethical guidelines.
    c.   Ethics are important in personal counseling but not necessary in career counseling.
    d.   The National Career Development Association has developed its own set of ethics.

ANSWER KEY

1.	b	11.	a	Q6.	F	Q16.	a
2.	c	12.	a	Q7.	T	Q17.	a
3.	a	13.	b	Q8.	F	Q18.	b
4.	b	14.	a	Q9.	F	Q19.	b
5.	c			Q10.	T	Q20.	c
6.	d	Q1.	T	Q11.	c	Q21.	b
7.	b	Q2.	T	Q12.	c	Q22.	d
8.	b	Q3.	T	Q13.	a	Q23.	b
9.	c	Q4.	F	Q14.	a	Q24.	b
10.	a	Q5.	T	Q15.	d	Q25.	c

CHAPTER 2
TRAIT AND FACTOR THEORY

Definition of trait

Definition of factor

Step 1: Gaining self understanding

   Aptitude

   Ability

   Achievement

   Interests

   Values

   Personality

Step 2: Obtaining knowledge about the world of work

   Types of occupational information

   Classification systems

     Holland's classification system

     Dictionary of Occupational Titles system

     Occupational Information Network (O*NET)

     Enhanced Guide for Occupational Exploration (GOE)

     Standard Occupational Classification Manual

Step 3: Integrating information about oneself and the world of work

   Test and inventory manuals matching patterns of scores

   Computer guidance systems

     SIGI[3]
     DISCOVER

Applying the theory to women

Applying the theory to culturally diverse populations

Counselor issues

CHAPTER 2

TRAIT AND FACTOR THEORY

EXERCISE 2.1

ABILITIES AND INTERESTS

Please rank the types of work that are listed below. You need only to rank your top 5, but can rank more if you wish. Assign a (1) to the type of work that you have the most interest in and sufficient aptitude or ability in to do it now or in the future. Assign a (2) to your second choice, and so forth. If you are not sure, you can guess. Some titles are general — you will be able to specify more clearly later. Use interest rather than ability as your primary guide in ranking these work activities. (This list is based on the *Guide for Occupational Exploration* (1979) that is shown in Table 2-8 [p.49] in the text.)

Artistic
__Literary Arts
__Visual Arts
__Performing arts: Drama
__Performing arts: Music
__Performing arts: Dance
__Crafts and arts
__Modeling

Scientific
__Physics, chemistry, geology, and similar
__Life sciences
__Medical sciences

Plants and Animals
__Managerial work with plants
__Managerial work with animals
__Animal training

Protective
__Law enforcement
__Security services

Mechanical
__Engineering
__Engineering technology
__Air and water vehicle transportation
__Quality control
__Land vehicle operation
__Equipment operation

Industrial
__Production technology
__Production work
__Quality control

Business Detail
__Administrative detail
__Mathematical detail

__Financial detail
__Processing records

Selling
__Technical sales
__General sales
__Vending

Accommodating
__Hospitality services
__Barber and beauty services
__Passenger services
__Customer services
__Attendant (such as flight)

Humanitarian
__Social services
__Nursing
__Teaching
__Child and adult care

Leading and Influencing
__Mathematics and statistics
__Education administration
__Library services
__Social research
__Law
__Business administration
__Finance
__Services administration
__Communications
__Marketing
__Enforcement of regulations

Physical Performing
__Sports
__Physical feats

11

EXERCISE 2.2

VALUES

Please rank the values that are listed below. Rank your top 5 (or more, if you wish). Assign a (1) to the value that is most important to you now. Assign a (2) to your second choice, and so forth. If you are not sure, you can guess. These are values that are related to work, rather than general life values.

__Advancing on a job
__Security in a job
__Being looked up to by others
__Being physically active
__Creating ideas and things
__Creating beauty
__Being independent
__Inventing new things
__Following directions
__Taking responsibility

__Having fun
__Helping people with personal problems
__Improving society
__Taking risks
__Designing systems
__Making money
__Organizing data
__Organizing things
__Having good working conditions
__Working on your own

EXERCISE 2.3

FINDING OCCUPATIONS THAT MATCH YOUR ABILITIES, INTERESTS, AND VALUES

E. 1. Use the rankings that you made in Exercises 2.1 and 2.2 to identify careers. Please write your highest rankings on the lines below.

_____

_____

_____

_____

E. 2. Turn to tables 2.6, 2.7, and 2.9 in the text. These occupational classification systems are similar to the one used in Exercise 2.1, but are longer. Use one or more of these to identify careers that you feel will fit your interests, abilities, values, and personality. If you need more information about an occupation, you can consult the *Occupational Outlook Handbook,* the *Dictionary of Occupational Titles* or the *O*NET.*

_____

_____

_____

_____

12

E. 3. What important aspects of your views of your career choice are included in this quick approach to finding a career choice?

_____

_____

_____

E. 4. What important aspects of your views of your career choice are NOT included in this quick approach to finding a career choice?

_____

_____

_____

HELPING DEION USING TRAIT AND FACTOR THEORY

In the following example, I will use the case of Deion to help you become familiar with trait and factor theory. Deion is a high school senior who is trying to decide whether or not to pursue college and what type of career to pursue. Each question helps to illustrate important concepts used in trait and factor theory.

1. Deion is confused by all of the career options that he has for next year. Using trait and factor theory, one of the first things that you would want to discuss with him is

    a.   his after school job.
    b.   his view of his teacher's attitudes towards higher education.
    c.   self assessment.
    d.   the labor market.

2. When talking about his enjoyment of the painting and drawing classes that he has attended in school and after school, Deion would be describing his

    a.   abilities.
    b.   interests.
    c.   personality.
    d.   values.

3. Deion won an award for a painting that he submitted to a contest at an art school in his neighborhood. This award can best be seen as an indication of art

    a.   achievement.
    b.   aptitude.
    c.   interest.
    d.   value.

4. Deion's artistic achievement can also be seen as potential for a successful career in art. If so, this could be an example of artistic

    a.   aptitude.
    b.   interest.
    c.   knowledge.
    d.   value.

5. Deion wants to be involved in creating beauty and in creating paintings and objects that others will enjoy. This is an example of Deion's artistic

    a.   ability.
    b.   interest.
    c.   knowledge.
    d.   values.

6. Deion enjoys doing many things in addition to art. He likes chemistry and physics as well as his English courses. He also enjoys helping his mother out in her grocery store. He wants to know how his likes and dislikes compare with people in different professions. He would find the following to be most helpful.

    a.   ability test
    b.   interest inventory
    c.   personality inventory
    d.   values inventory

After talking with you and reviewing his interests, abilities, personality, and values, Deion takes appropriate inventories. You go over the results with him and he decides to explore different occupations. He then starts to consider how to learn about different occupations.

7. You think about occupations using the concepts of data, persons, and things with Deion. These concepts are most closely associated with the

    a.   Dictionary of Occupational Titles.
    b.   Guide for Occupational Exploration System.
    c.   O*NET (the Occupational Information Network).
    d.   Standard Occupational Classification System.

8. One of the following classification systems is not being revised and, although it can be useful, runs the risk of being out of date. You decide not to use the _____ with Deion.

    a.   Dictionary of Occupational Titles
    b.   Guide for Occupational Exploration System
    c.   O*NET (the Occupational Information Network)
    d.   Standard Occupational Classification System

9. You decide to give Deion some reading assignments from a book that is relatively easy to use and that uses a classification system that is easy to understand. Which of the following would you use?

    a.   Dictionary of Occupational Titles
    b.   Guide for Occupational Exploration System
    c.   O*NET (the Occupational Information Network)
    d.   Standard Occupational Classification System

10. A good resource for Deion to use in learning about careers is

    a.   a resume writing book.
    b.   Sharf's *Applying Career Development Theory to Counseling.*
    c.   *The Occupational Outlook Handbook.*
    d.   want ads.

11. When Deion has completed his self-assessment and learned about occupations related to the self-assessment, he is ready for this aspect of trait and factor theory.

    a.   getting better grades in school
    b.   integrating information about himself and occupations
    c.   going to college to get a better job
    d.   differentiating his knowledge about occupations

12. Using the trait and factor model, if Deion is not sure about which occupations he may enter after high school graduation, you may

    a.   suggest that he go to college.
    b.   continue to do self assessment and explore occupations.
    c.   request a parent teacher conference.
    d.   assign him to another counselor.

APPLYING TRAIT AND FACTOR THEORY TO WOMEN AND CULTURALLY DIVERSE GROUPS

Does trait and factor theory have different implications for men and women? Explain.

_____

_____

_____

_____

_____

_____

_____

_____

15

What implications does trait and factor theory have for counseling people from diverse populations?

_____

_____

_____

_____

STRENGTHS AND LIMITATIONS

What do you see as the strengths and limitations of trait and factor theory?

Strengths   Limitations

_____   _____

_____   _____

_____   _____

_____   _____

_____

TRAIT AND FACTOR THEORY: A QUIZ

True or false items: Decide if the following items are more "true" or more "false" as they apply to concepts discussed in this chapter.

T   F   Q1.   An early career development theory, trait and factor theory continues to have an important impact on other career development theories.

T   F   Q2.   The first step in trait and factor theory is to provide occupational information to the client.

T   F   Q3.   To determine the level of competence that a mechanical engineer has, it would be appropriate to give her an aptitude test.

T   F   Q4.   Interests in activities can be measured, but interests that compare a person's interests to people in a specific field can NOT be measured.

T   F   Q5.   Values inventories predict success in occupational endeavors.

T   F   Q6.   Assessing one's personality is important in personal counseling but is not relevant in career counseling.

16

T F Q7. Occupational classification systems have been developed to organize the large number of occupations that exist.

T F Q8. The O*NET was developed to replace the Guide for Occupational Exploration System.

T F Q9. Integrating information about self and the world of work is an essential aspect of trait and factor theory.

T F Q10. Classification systems classify most occupations, rather than just a few major occupations.

Multiple choice items: Select the best answer from the alternatives given. Answer each question from the point of view of work adjustment theory.

Q11. Which of the following is NOT a part of trait and factor theory?

   a.   ability
   b.   empathy
   c.   interests
   d.   values

Q12. According to trait and factor theory, seniors in high school should

   a.   assess their interests, abilities, and values.
   b.   get a part time job in high school.
   c.   follow the suggestions of parents in choosing a career.
   d.   go to college to get a high paying job.

Q13. Which of the following shows that students have potential for doing tasks well in their chosen field?

   a.   aptitude tests
   b.   achievement tests
   c.   personality inventories
   d.   value inventories

Q14. A test that measures knowledge of real estate sales is most likely to be a(an)

   a.   aptitude test.
   b.   achievement test.
   c.   interest inventory.
   d.   personality inventory.

Q15. Enjoying selling real estate is most likely to be indicated on a(an)

   a.   aptitude test.
   b.   achievement test.
   c.   interest inventory.
   d.   personality inventory.

17

Q16.   Which of the following has no right or wrong answers?

    a.   ability test
    b.   aptitude test
    c.   achievement test
    d.   interest inventory

Q17.   Which of these is least likely to contain occupational information?

    a.   book
    b.   brochure
    c.   inventory
    d.   web page

Q18.   An occupational crosswalk is a

    a.   cross-reference to another classification system.
    b.   crossing guard at a school.
    c.   crossword puzzle with occupational clues.
    d.   reference to another source of occupational information.

Q19.   Data, persons, and things are categories that are central to this classification system.

    a.   Dictionary of Occupational Titles
    b.   Guide for Occupational Exploration System
    c.   O*NET
    d.   Standard Occupational Classification System

Q20.   Which occupational classification system is based on interest categories?

    a.   Dictionary of Occupational Titles
    b.   Guide for Occupational Exploration System
    c.   O*NET
    d.   Standard Occupational Classification System

Q21.   An advantage that computer guidance systems have over inventories and tests is that they are

    a.   cheaper.
    b.   more reliable.
    c.   more valid.
    d.   interactive.

Q22.   Which of the following occupational titles would be inappropriate when describing someone's occupation?

    a.   judge
    b.   mailman
    c.   secretary
    d.   truck driver

Q23. Which age group is least likely to be appropriate for trait and factor theory?

    a.   8 to 10
    b.   18 to 20
    c.   48 to 50
    d.   68 to 70

Q24. Trait and factor theory is best known for its use of

    a.   assessment instruments.
    b.   directive counseling.
    c.   school personnel in leading career classes.
    d.   occupational classification systems.

Q25. Mariah wants to be a nurse because she hears that there are many job openings in the health field. A trait and factor career counselor would be concerned that Mariah did not consider her

    a.   abilities, interests, and values.
    b.   counselor's advice.
    c.   knowledge about the nursing profession.
    d.   use of occupational classifications systems.

ANSWER KEY

1.	c	11.	b	Q8.	F	Q18.	a
2.	b	12.	b	Q9.	T	Q19.	a
3.	a			Q10.	T	Q20.	b
4.	a	Q1.	T	Q11.	b	Q21.	d
5.	d	Q2.	F	Q12.	a	Q22.	b
6.	b	Q3.	F	Q13.	a	Q23.	a
7.	a	Q4.	F	Q14.	b	Q24.	a
8.	a	Q5.	F	Q15.	c	Q25.	a
9.	b	Q6.	F	Q16.	d		
10.	c	Q7.	T	Q17.	c		

CHAPTER 3
OCCUPATIONS: INFORMATION AND THEORY

The United States labor market

Human capital theory

Sociological and economic approaches

The structure of the labor market

Youth employment

Women and discrimination in the workplace

Gender segregation

The effect of the work on the individual

**Culturally diverse individuals and
discrimination in the workplace**

Status attainment theory

CHAPTER 3

OCCUPATIONS: INFORMATION AND THEORY

EXERCISE 3.1

SOCIOLOGICAL AND ECONOMIC PERSPECTIVES ON YOUR CAREER DEVELOPMENT

E. 1. When you were in high school, what were the reasons that you worked part-time or did volunteer work? (If you list "to make money", explain what you needed to make money for. List other reasons as well.) (Youth Employment)

_____

_____

_____

_____

_____

E. 2. What did you learn from part-time or volunteer work in high school? (Youth Employment)

_____

_____

_____

_____

E. 3. If you stayed at the worst job that you ever had for 50 years, would that affect your intellectual ability? Explain. (The Effect of the Work Environment on the Individual)

_____

_____

_____

_____

21

E. 4. In choosing an occupation, how important is prestige to you? What jobs would you not take because others do not value them? (Status Attainment Theory)

_____

_____

_____

_____

E. 5. Did your family encourage you to go to college? How was this related to the prestige level of your father's occupation? (Status Attainment Theory)

_____

_____

_____

_____

E. 6. Comment on the accuracy of this statement: "I have invested in my education and training to increase my life time earnings". (Human Capital Theory)

_____

_____

_____

_____

E. 7. Comment on the accuracy of this statement: "I have invested in my education and training to increase my enjoyment of my career". (Human Capital Theory)

_____

_____

_____

_____

E. 8. How did the different jobs that you have had vary in the opportunities for advancement, job stability, and high salary? (The Structure of the Labor Market)

_____

_____

_____

_____

_____

E. 9. How have you experienced or observed (or heard about), the discrimination of women in the workplace? (Women and Discrimination in the Workplace)

_____

_____

_____

_____

E. 10. How have you experienced or observed (or heard about), the discrimination of people from culturally diverse groups in the workplace? (Culturally Diverse Individuals and Discrimination in the Workplace)

_____

_____

_____

_____

_____

COUNSELOR STATEMENTS THAT REFLECT SOCIOLOGICAL AND ECONOMIC THEORIES

In each of the following questions, a client statement will be given. A counselor statement will follow the remark by the client. You will be asked to identify the correct sociological or economic theory or approach that best represents or describes the client-counselor dialogue.

1. CL: I am thinking about being a doctor. That is one of the occupations that my parents think highly of.

    CO: Parental influence can be an important factor in choosing a career. Is that true for you?
    a.   effect of the work environment on the individual
    b.   human capital theory
    c.   status attainment theory
    d.   the structure of the labor market

2. CL: I have been working for a company for two years where all I do is sort out flower bulbs by their size. I feel like I can't talk to my friends the way I used to be able to.

    CO: You are concerned that you aren't learning new things and can't express yourself intellectually the way you would like.

    a.   effect of the work environment on the individual
    b.   human capital theory
    c.   status attainment theory
    d.   the structure of the labor market

3. CL: I am working for this new fast food restaurant that pays two dollars more per hour than minimum wage. I am thinking of dropping out of high school at the end of my junior year so I can make good money at that restaurant.

    CO: Have you thought about how that decision could affect your salary in ten years?

    a.   effect of the work environment on the individual
    b.   human capital theory
    c.   status attainment theory
    d.   the structure of the labor market

4. CL: I am a biology major in my junior year of college. I don't have enough money to go to medical school after college so I plan to sell cars for two years so I can finance my medical school education.

    CO: You seem to have made a clear decision to invest in your future career.
    a.   effect of the work environment on the individual
    b.   human capital theory
    c.   status attainment theory
    d.   the structure of the labor market

5. CL: When my mother went back to work after taking care of my sister and me, she didn't return to her teaching job, but took a job as a cashier. That bothered me. I want to make sure I advance and make something of myself.

   CO: Having a job where you feel respected is important. Having your mother go backwards in terms of the prestige level of her work bothered you.

      a.   effect of the work environment on the individual
      b.   human capital theory
      c.   status attainment theory
      d.   the structure of the labor market

6. CL: When I graduate from college next month, I know that I can get a job at this credit card company I work for now. I think I would like to get a Master's of Business Administration degree so that I can advance into management more quickly.

   CO: You seem to be thinking into the future and making an investment into having a greater salary in a few years.

      a.   effect of the work environment on the individual
      b.   human capital theory
      c.   status attainment theory
      d.   the structure of the labor market

7. CL: My father has been doing manual labor, mainly setting fences into the ground, for the past ten years. Not only does it tire him physically, but also it is harder to talk to him about things that affect my future and moving away to school.

   CO: It's hard to see your father not be able to talk with you the way he used to.

      a.   effect of the work environment on the individual
      b.   human capital theory
      c.   status attainment theory
      d.   the structure of the labor market

8. CL: I thought I was so much better off than my friends because I was earning money while they were spending money for college. Now I am working in this clothing store. I keep being passed over for management jobs while other people that I used to work with have a college degree and are store managers making more than twice the money that I am making.

   CO: It can be really hard to move from one type of job to another in certain types of work.

      a.   effect of the work environment on the individual
      b.   human capital theory
      c.   status attainment theory
      d.   the structure of the labor market

POSSIBLE STUDENT QUESTIONS ABOUT EMPLOYMENT AND DISCRIMINATION

If you are or will be a counselor dealing with career issues, you may be asked questions by students about the labor market or discrimination. Using the choices below, please answer questions that students might ask which are covered in the text.

9. What jobs seem to be growing most and are most likely to have opportunities for entry?

    a.   agricultural jobs
    b.   manufacturing
    c.   mining
    d.   professional specialty areas

10. Is it harder to get a job with some high school education than with a bachelor's degree?

    a.   No, the opportunities for both groups are about equal.
    b.   No, there are more jobs for those with some high school education.
    c.   Yes, the rate of participation in the labor force is significantly higher for those with a bachelor's degree than for those with some high school education.
    d.   Yes, the rate of participation in the labor force for those with some high school education is below 20%.

11. In general, do women earn as much as men?

    a.   No, men tend to earn more than women do. The percentage depends on the ethnic group.
    b.   No, men earn about twice what women do, regardless of ethnic group.
    c.   Yes, there are equal opportunities for women who therefore receive equal pay.
    d.   Yes, since women tend to enter occupations that require more education than men, they receive more than men.

12. Do young African Americans have more difficulty getting employment than Caucasian youth?

    a.   No, there is no racial discrimination in employment.
    b.   No, laws make it possible for equal employment among all youth.
    c.   Yes, African Americans have more difficulty finding jobs than Caucasian youth.
    d.   Yes, African American and Asian youth have more difficulty finding jobs than Caucasian youth.

13. Does discrimination for advancing in a job in the United States still occur?

    a.   No, there is no racial discrimination among employers.
    b.   Rarely, this only occurs in small firms.
    c.   Rarely, this only occurs in certain states in the United States.
    d.   Yes, people from culturally diverse populations may have more difficulty advancing than Caucasian individuals.

26

STRENGTHS AND LIMITATIONS

In general, what do you see as the strengths and limitations of sociological and economic approaches to career counseling?

        Strengths   Limitations

_____   _____

_____   _____

_____   _____

_____   _____

OCCUPATIONS: INFORMATION AND THEORY: A QUIZ

True or false items: Decide if the following items are more "true" or more "false" as they apply to concepts discussed in this chapter.

T F   Q1. In the U.S. economy, more job openings will be due to replacement needs than to growth.

T F   Q2. In the U.S. economy, there is likely to be more growth in manufacturing than service jobs.

T F   Q3. In the U.S. economy, earnings are unrelated to amount of years of employee education.

T F   Q4. Compared to older individuals, youth are more likely to be unemployed and underemployed.

T F   Q5. Complex work can help individuals deal with complex tasks that they may encounter in later working situations.

T F   Q6. The best predictor of later occupational success is the number of siblings an individual has.

T F   Q7. As explained in the text, human capital theory is based on the idea that employers invest in the economic worth of their employees.

T F   Q8. Human capital theory assumes that the labor market is open to all individuals on an equal basis.

T F   Q9. The structure of the labor market is one that has segments. It can be difficult to move from one segment to another.

T F   Q10. Evidence exists that shows that in the U.S., when Caucasians and African Americans have similar resumes, African Americans experience more discrimination in employment.

Multiple choice items: Select the best answer from the alternatives given. Answer each question from the point of view of sociological and economic perspectives on the labor market.

Q11.   Which of these occupations is NOT one of the fast growing occupations in the U.S. economy?

    a.   database administrators
    b.   farmers
    c.   medical assistants
    d.   physical therapists

Q12.   Individuals with a bachelor's degree earn, on average, _____ as individuals who do not graduate from high school.

    a.   about the same
    b.   half as much
    c.   eight times as much
    d.   twice as much

Q13.   Substantive complexity of work can directly increase one's

    a.   energy.
    b.   interests.
    c.   level of intellectual functioning.
    d.   opportunities for advancement.

Q14.   In research on status attainment theory, mother's occupation has been found to be a(an)

    a.   an important predictor of son or daughter's career choice.
    b.   not an important predictor of son or daughter's career choice.
    c.   factor related to individuals career decision-making style.
    d.   factor related to holistic adjustment to work.

Q15.   Using status attainment theory, a counselor may wish to

    a.   encourage students to value the importance of prestige in career choice.
    b.   encourage students who do not have parents with highly prestigious jobs to strive to achieve despite parental background.
    c.   help students realize that intellectually challenging jobs can lead to better paying jobs.
    d.   warn students about the hazards of pursuing jobs that do not fit in with goals of individuals in their own social strata.

Q16.   To view your own education as a financial investment in a future career is consistent with

    a.   general trait and factor theory.
    b.   human capital theory.
    c.   status attainment theory.
    d.   the structure of the labor market.

Q17.	Modern human capital theory sees as an acceptable goal for individual investment,

a.	helping others.
b.	improving spiritual balance.
c.	finding a calling.
d.	risk taking.

Q18.	Being unable to move from one general type of work to another is discussed by this approach.

a.	trait and factor theory
b.	human capital
c.	status attainment
d.	the structure of the labor market

Q19.	The structure of labor markets in different countries tends

a.	to have fewer sectors than are found in the United States.
b.	to have more sectors than are found in the United States.
c.	to have structures unique to their own economies.
d.	to be similar to that of the United States.

Q20.	Which of the following is an example of a type of discrimination that women may experience when looking for employment?

a.	balance discrimination
b.	mandatory discrimination
c.	irresponsible discrimination
d.	statistical discrimination

Q21.	In general, unemployment rates in the United States tend to differ

a.	more by gender than by race.
b.	more by race than by gender.
c.	equally by race and gender.
d.	very little by race or gender.

Q22.	In the study of work, gender segregation refers to

a.	employment discrimination against women.
b.	earnings discrimination against women.
c.	sexual harassment laws.
d.	the distribution of men and women in different occupations.

Q23.	Ogbu believed that the experience of African Americans in the work force and in career choice can be different than other minority groups because African Americans can be seen as a (an)

a.	involuntary minority group.
b.	new majority group.
c.	vocal minority group.
d.	voluntary minority group.

29

Q24.   In counseling individuals from culturally diverse groups, counselors should be aware of their own

    a.   attitudes towards their agency.
    b.   attitudes towards their clients.
    c.   views of the structure of the labor market.
    d.   views on status attainment theory.

Q25.   Status attainment theory is an example of a (an)

    a.   economic theory.
    b.   philosophical theory.
    c.   psychological theory.
    d.   sociological theory.

ANSWER KEY

1.	c	11.	a	Q8.	T	Q18.	d
2.	a	12.	c	Q9.	T	Q19.	c
3.	d	13.	d	Q10.	T	Q20.	d
4.	b			Q11.	b	Q21.	b
5.	c	Q1.	T	Q12.	d	Q22.	d
6.	b	Q2.	F	Q13.	c	Q23.	a
7.	a	Q3.	F	Q14.	b	Q24.	b
8.	d	Q4.	T	Q15.	b	Q25.	d
9.	d	Q5.	T	Q16.	b		
10.	c	Q6.	F	Q17.	a		
		Q7.	F				

CHAPTER 4
WORK ADJUSTMENT THEORY

Definition of work adjustment

Definition of satisfaction

Definition of satisfactoriness

Step 1: Assessing abilities, values, personality, and interests

Abilities — GATB
    General learning ability
    Verbal ability
    Numerical ability
    Spatial ability
    Form perception
    Clerical ability
    Eye/hand coordination
    Finger dexterity
    Manual dexterity

Values (20 needs are grouped within 6 values in the Minnesota Importance Questionnaire)

    Achievement
        Ability utilization
        Achievement
    Comfort
        Activity
        Independence
        Variety
        Compensation
        Security
        Working Conditions
    Status
        Advancement
        Recognition
        Authority
        Social status
        Coworkers
    Altruism
        Moral values
        Social service
    Safety
        Company policies and practices
        Supervision - Human relations
        Supervision - Technical

    Autonomy
        Creativity
        Responsibility

Personality styles
    Celerity
    Pace
    Rhythm
    Endurance

Interests develop from values and abilities

Step 2: Measuring the requirements and conditions of occupations

Ability Patterns (GATB)

Value patterns (Minnesota Job Description Questionnaire)

Combining ability and value patterns (Minnesota Occupational Classification System)

Step 3: Matching abilities, values, and reinforcers

Use MIQ, GATB, MOCS

Adjustment style
    Flexibility
    Activeness
    Reactiveness
    Perseverance

Job adjustment counseling

Adjustment to retirement

New developments

The role of assessment instruments

Applying the theory to women and culturally diverse populations

Counselor issues

31

CHAPTER 4

WORK ADJUSTMENT THEORY

EXERCISE 4.1

WORK NEEDS AND JOBS

E. 1. Rank the five needs that are most important to you in working on a job. Assign the number (1) to the most important and the number (2) to the next most important, and so forth.

_____ Use your abilities
_____ Get a feeling of accomplishment
_____ Keep busy all the time
_____ Do different activities
_____ Get paid well compared to your colleagues
_____ Have steady employment
_____ Have good working conditions
_____ Be able to get promoted
_____ Be recognized for what you do
_____ Tell others what to do
_____ Be looked up to by others
_____ Have friends on the job
_____ Do morally acceptable work
_____ Be treated fairly by the company
_____ Have a supervisor who is on your side
_____ Work where you and others are trained well
_____ Try out your new ideas
_____ Make decisions about your work

E. 2. List three different jobs that you have had and the needs that they met for you. (Choose the needs from the above list). In the list of needs below, circle those that you ranked in the top five above.

Jobs	Needs
1. _____	_____
2. _____	_____
3. _____	_____

E. 3. Why is each of the needs that are in your top five important to you?

_____

_____

_____

32

E. 4. List three occupations that meet most of the needs in your list of top five needs.

_____

_____

E. 5. Why is it important to you to meet your needs in your work?

_____

_____

_____

ASSESSING ABILITIES, VALUES, PERSONALITY, AND INTERESTS

The following case study provides a means for testing your knowledge about how work adjustment theory addresses the concepts of abilities, values, personality, and interests.

Mort, age 32, is a carpenter who has been in the hospital due to a construction accident. Although he has recovered from back surgery, he will not be able to lift heavy weights again. He has been seeking help for his worries about what he will do to assist in providing for his family. His wife has been at home caring for their two and four year old girls.

When Mort was in high school, he was a B student in a college prep program. Because he married soon after graduation from high school, he never felt he was able to go to college. He did well in both math and English courses in high school. In high school and during the last 13 years, he has enjoyed participating in and watching most team sports. Mort's mother was a nurse and his father worked in a steel mill as a laborer. Mort became interested in helping people who were disabled or had problems due to illness. Occasionally, Mort's mother would care for someone who was disabled and part of the care took place in his home. He had a sense of pride in helping his mother care for people. He also felt that it was work that was consistent with his moral values. Another aspect of health care work that he valued was the sense that his mother could use skills that she had learned. Nursing someone back to health was an accomplishment that he could take pride in. He felt the same sense of pride when he built part of a house. He was able to use his wood working skills and appreciate the quality of the finished project.

When Mort worked as a carpenter, he was not concerned about how quickly he got the job done (celerity); however, he was concerned about how he felt about his effort (pace). Mort did not like to be interrupted in his work, but preferred to work steadily until a job was done (rhythm). Mort is now concerned that he is unable to have the energy to work on tasks, particularly ones that require physical labor (endurance). A question that concerns Mort is whether or not he will be able to be as effective a worker as he once was.

1. If you are Mort's counselor and making use of work adjustment theory, which approach are you likely to take in assessing Mort's abilities?

    a.   Assess Mort's abilities by reviewing what others have said about his skills.
    b.   Assign the General Aptitude Test Battery or Ability Profiler to Mort.
    c.   Ignore his abilities and focus on personality.
    d.   Review his high school grades.

33

2. Having good grades in school would be an example of Mort's

   a.   ability.
   b.   interests.
   c.   values.
   d.   work adjustment.

3. Two of Mort's needs that he may wish to satisfy in a future career are

   a.   ability utilization, achievement.
   b.   advancement, recognition.
   c.   compensation, security.
   d.   variety, working conditions.

4. Mort's concern about not being able to have the energy or ability to work as he used to is an example of

   a.   ability patterns.
   b.   adjustment style.
   c.   personality style.
   d.   value patterns.

5. To measure Mort's values from a work adjustment theory perspective, a counselor is likely to use

   a.   The Minnesota Importance Questionnaire.
   b.   The Minnesota Job Description Questionnaire.
   c.   The Minnesota Occupational Classification System.
   d.   The Values Scale.

6. Mort's lack of concern about being creative in his work is a reflection of a limited amount of a

   a.   specific ability.
   b.   specific interest.
   c.   specific need.
   d.   value range.

7. Using work adjustment theory with Mort, which of these are you most likely to focus on in your counseling sessions with him?

   a.   adjustment style
   b.   interest patterns
   c.   personality style
   d.   value patterns

MEASURING THE REQUIREMENTS AND CONDITIONS OF OCCUPATIONS

For the purpose of the next three questions, imagine that you wish to add the occupation of web designer to the Minnesota Occupational Classification System. You will need to collect information about the occupation so that you can develop a means of assessing whether a client might be an appropriate fit for the occupation.

8. Which instrument would you use to measure the ability of a group of web designers?

      a.   General Aptitude Test Battery or Ability Profiler
      b.   Minnesota Importance Questionnaire
      c.   Minnesota Job Description Questionnaire
      d.   Personality Styles Instruments

9. Which instrument would you use to measure the values of a group of web designers?

      a.   General Aptitude Test Battery
      b.   Minnesota Importance Questionnaire
      c.   Minnesota Job Description Questionnaire
      d.   Personality Styles Instrument

10. Where would you want to put the profile that you have developed on web designers?

      a.   Dictionary of Occupational Titles
      b.   Minnesota Occupational Classification System
      c.   Occupational Outlook Handbook
      d.   O*NET

JOB ADJUSTMENT COUNSELING

Nora works as a sales person in a furniture store. She has been selling furniture for the last four years. She would like to move to a management position. She no longer gets the feeling of accomplishment in selling living room and bedroom sets that she used to. Her manager, Lara, feels that Nora's sales have been dropping off because she does not seem to have the same enthusiasm for selling as she did the last few years.

11. As a counselor using work adjustment theory, you would attend to Nora's

      a.   needs that no longer are being met.
      b.   conflict with Lara.
      c.   score on the GATB or Ability Profiler.
      d.   information from the MOCS.

12. Lara is most concerned with Nora's productivity and thus is concerned about her

      a.   interests.
      b.   job satisfaction.
      c.   satisfactoriness.
      d.   values.

13. Nora is most concerned about her own

    a.   earnings.
    b.   job satisfaction.
    c.   interests.
    d.   satisfactoriness.

APPLYING WORK ADJUSTMENT THEORY TO WOMEN AND CULTURALLY DIVERSE GROUPS

Does this theory have different implications for men and women? Explain.

_____

_____

_____

_____

What implications does work adjustment theory have for counseling people from diverse populations?

_____

_____

_____

_____

STRENGTHS AND LIMITATIONS

What do you see as the strengths and limitations of work adjustment theory?

           Strengths   Limitations

_____   _____

_____   _____

_____   _____

_____   _____

_____   _____

WORK ADJUSTMENT THEORY: A QUIZ

True or false items: Decide if the following items are more "true" or more "false" as they apply to concepts discussed in this chapter.

T   F   Q1. Work adjustment theory was designed to help high school students make career choices.

T   F   Q2. An employer's view of an employee's work performance in work adjustment theory is referred to as satisfactoriness.

T   F   Q3. In the Minnesota Importance Questionnaire each scale is represented by only one item.

T   F   Q4. Results of the Minnesota Importance Questionnaire are organized so that need scales are grouped into six values.

T   F   Q5 Occupational Interest Patterns are a part of work adjustment theory.

T   F   Q6. Minnesota Job Description Questionnaires are used to assess an individual's values and needs.

T   F   Q7. Assessing how a person's values and needs are being met by their work is one of the most important concepts that counselors attend to in work adjustment counseling.

T   F   Q8. When doing retirement counseling using work adjustment theory, assessing how new activities serve as reinforcers for an individual is an important aspect of the counseling process.

T   F   Q9. The Minnesota Importance Questionnaire contains value and ability patterns for 1769 occupations.

T   F   Q10. There are different occupational reinforcer patterns for specific occupations based on ethnicity

Multiple choice items: Select the best answer from the alternatives given. Answer each question from the point of view of work adjustment theory.

Q11.   Which of the following concepts from work adjustment theory refers to an employer's view of an employee's performance?

   a.   ability patterns
   b.   satisfaction
   c.   satisfactoriness
   d.   value patterns

37

Q12. Which of the following is NOT one of the six values that are important to work adjustment theory?

    a.   altruism
    b.   autonomy
    c.   spirituality
    d.   status

Q13. In work adjustment theory, safety refers to

    a.   company and supervisory relationships.
    b.   absence of hazards at work.
    c.   job security.
    d.   having security officers on the premises.

Q14. Using work adjustment theory, safety refers to

    a.   family support systems.
    b.   income.
    c.   physical health.
    d.   values.

Q15. The way that counselors who use work adjustment theory are most likely to measure clients' abilities is to

    a.   ask former employers.
    b.   get self-estimates of ability from clients.
    c.   use a test of abilities.
    d.   use high school or college grades.

Q16. Which of these is NOT a personality style according to work adjustment theory?

    a.   celerity
    b.   endurance
    c.   rigidity
    d.   rhythm

Q17. In work adjustment theory, personality styles refer to how

    a.   people get along at work.
    b.   people relate to members of their own family.
    c.   scores on the Minnesota Multiphasic Personality Inventory reflect individual's personalities.
    d.   the abilities and values of individuals interact with their work tasks.

Q18. According to work adjustment theory, Harry's interests in biology are

    a.   derived from his abilities and values.
    b.   derived from scores on interest inventories.
    c.   inherited from his father.
    d.   learned at school.

Q19. The Minnesota Job Description Questionnaire measures patterns of _____ that are found in the workplace.

    a.   ability
    b.   supervision
    c.   required tasks
    d.   values

Q20. In work adjustment theory, individuals' values and abilities are matched with

    a.   patterns of abilities and values found in different occupations.
    b.   job descriptions in want ads.
    c.   Dictionary of Occupational Titles and O*NET descriptions of occupations.
    d.   patterns of interests and personality found in different occupations.

Q21. A retired worker wishing to spend some time teaching children, is most likely to have the work adjustment theory value of

    a.   altruism.
    b.   extraversion.
    c.   safety.
    d.   spirituality.

Q22. In addition to using work adjustment theory to understand the behavior of working adults, work adjustment theory has also been applied to

    a.   children in sixth grade.
    b.   political behavior.
    c.   prison populations.
    d.   young gifted adolescents.

Q23. In work adjustment theory, adjustment styles refer to how individuals relate to the

    a.   behavior of supervisors.
    b.   idea of seeking counseling for work adjustment problems.
    c.   occupational environment.
    d.   value patterns that describe them.

Q24. Work adjustment theory can be applied to

    a.   labor market trends.
    b.   political forecasting.
    c.   setting wage policies.
    d.   sexual harassment and discrimination problems.

Q25. In work adjustment theory, counselors can see themselves and their clients as

    a.   ability patterns.
    b.   collaborators working together.
    c.   reinforcers for each other.
    d.   value patterns.

39

ANSWER KEY

1.	b	11.	a	Q6.	F	Q16.	c
2.	a	12.	c	Q7.	T	Q17.	d
3.	a	13.	b	Q8.	T	Q18.	a
4.	c			Q9.	F	Q19.	d
5.	a			Q10.	F	Q20.	a
6.	c	Q1.	F	Q11.	c	Q21.	a
7.	d	Q2.	T	Q12.	c	Q22.	d
8.	a	Q3.	T	Q13.	a	Q23.	c
9.	c	Q4.	T	Q14.	d	Q24.	d
10.	b	Q5.	F	Q15.	c	Q25.	c

40

CHAPTER 5
HOLLAND'S THEORY OF TYPES

Career choice and career adjustment represents an extension of personality

Stereotypes — People's impressions and generalizations about work

Holland assigns people and work environments to specific categories
Realistic.

Investigative

Artistic

Social

Enterprising

Conventional

Combination of types

Explanatory constructs

Congruence

Differentiation

Consistency

Identity

Research on Holland's constructs

Role of occupational information

The role of assessment instruments

Applying the theory to women

Applying the theory to culturally diverse populations

Counselor issues

CHAPTER 5
HOLLAND'S THEORY OF TYPES

EXERCISE 5.1

PERSONALITY TYPE AND OCCUPATIONS

Please rank the six boxes of activities and the six boxes of occupations that you like best. Rank each group in each column from 1 to 6 on the next page, with 1 being the best fit and 6 being the poorest fit. It is not necessary that you like all or most characteristics or occupations in a group to rank them highly.

ACTIVITIES	OCCUPATIONS
Group R	**Group R**
Practical Like to fix things Like outdoor work Work with your hands Like mechanical things	Carpenter Military officer Mechanic Bus or truck driver Electrician
Group I	**Group I**
Solve puzzles or problems Enjoy learning new things Like science Like math	Computer programmer Biologist Physician Mathematician
Group A	**Group A**
Play music Draw Act in a play Make recipes Write stories	Artist Movie director Chef Author Musician
Group S	**Group S**
Teach others Help others with personal problems Think through ethical issues Resolve personal conflicts	Teacher Social worker Ethicist Marriage counselor
Group E	**Group E**
Be assertive Persuade others Act self confidently Be a leader Manage others	Real estate broker Store manager Politician Executive Buyer

ACTIVITIES	OCCUPATIONS
Group C	**Group C**
Be dependable	Office manager
Follow rules	Accountant
Manage money	Bookkeeper
Use numbers	Banker
Accomplish tasks in an organized way	Credit manager

List the letters of the six groups of activities and occupations from 1 to 6 (1 is the best fit, 6 the poorest fit).

        Activities   **Occupations**

1. _____ _____
2. _____ _____
3. _____ _____
4. _____ _____
5. _____ _____
6. _____ _____

E. 1. How similar are your activities list and your occupations list? _____Why?

_____

_____

_____

E. 2. Explain how well these activities represent aspects of your personality.

_____

_____

_____

E. 3. Explain how well these six categories of occupations represent your career choices.

_____

_____

_____

E. 4. Can you think of a seventh category of activities or occupations? _____ What is it?

_____

E. 5. How well does your current occupational choice fit with the occupations in your most highly ranked group? _____ Explain.

_____

_____

_____

HOLLAND'S TYPES IN COUNSELING

In the following example, I will use the case of Niki to help you become familiar with Holland's theory. Niki is a high school junior who is trying to decide whether or not to pursue college and what type of career she should pursue. Each question helps to further develop information about her interests and abilities. The first six questions concern Holland's types, and the next six relate to the explanatory constructs of congruence, differentiation, consistency, and identity.

1. Niki is very much enjoying the chemistry course that she has now and the geology course she had freshman year. This indicates an interest in which of the following Holland types?

    a.   Artistic
    b.   Investigative
    c.   Realistic
    d.   Social

2. She currently has an after school job in which she works on word processing programs, spread sheets, and photo copying. She finds this work to be boring. This working environment fits most closely with which of these Holland categories?

    a.   Artistic
    b.   Conventional
    c.   Enterprising
    d.   Social

3. Her father is a nurse who works in the emergency ward of a local hospital. She likes to listen to him describe the type of operations that take place in the emergency room where medical personnel try to diagnose the patients' problems. She enjoys talking to him about how he assists in operations. Her interests most closely fit with this Holland type.

    a.   Artistic
    b.   Investigative
    c.   Realistic
    d.   Social

4. Niki also enjoys music and plays the trombone in her high school band. During the spring she also participates in the high school jazz band. This activity most closely fits with this Holland type.

   a. Artistic
   b. Enterprising
   c. Realistic
   d. Social

5. Although Niki enjoys her time with friends, she does not feel that she wants to teach or help others with personal problems. Given this information, Niki would probably not like this Holland environment very much.

   a. Artistic
   b. Enterprising
   c. Realistic
   d. Social

6. When Niki's mother takes apart their computer to fix it or to add parts, Niki can't understand how her mother can enjoy this activity. This activity is best described by this Holland type.

   a. Artistic
   b. Conventional
   c. Enterprising
   d. Realistic

7. Niki appears to have interest in Investigative and Artistic types. According to Holland, these types are

   a. congruent.
   b. consistent.
   c. differentiated.
   d. undifferentiated.

8. Niki's interests in only Artistic and Investigative activities can be described as limited. Holland would describe this using what term?

   a. congruent
   b. incongruent
   c. differentiated
   d. undifferentiated

9. The emergency room where her father works is one in which surgery takes place around the clock. This environment can best be described as

   a. congruent.
   b. consistent.
   c. differentiated.
   d. undifferentiated.

10. Niki's Holland type appears to be quite _____ an emergency room environment.

    a.   congruent with
    b.   differentiated from
    c.   identified with
    d.   incongruent with

11. Currently, Niki is not sure of her career plan or her goals for future education. Which of these Holland concepts refers to her amount of certainty?

    a.   congruent
    b.   consistent
    c.   differentiated
    d.   identity

12. The occupation of physical therapist is likely to be _____ Niki's future career plan.

    a.   congruent with
    b.   differentiated from
    c.   consistent with
    d.   incongruent with

APPLYING HOLLAND'S THEORY TO WOMEN AND CULTURALLY DIVERSE GROUPS

Does this theory have different implications for men and women? Explain.

_____

_____

_____

_____

_____

What implications does Holland's theory have for counseling people from diverse populations?

_____

_____

_____

_____

_____

STRENGTHS AND LIMITATIONS

What do you see as the strengths and limitations of Holland's theory?

Strengths	Limitations
_____	_____
_____	_____
_____	_____
_____	_____
_____	_____

HOLLAND'S THEORY: A QUIZ

True or false items: Decide if the following items are more "true" or more "false" as they apply to concepts discussed in this chapter?

T F Q1. Holland's theory is a specific type of trait and factor theory.

T F Q2. According to Holland, the following would be a good definition of the Social type: "Like to go to parties and socialize with others."

T F Q3. In Holland's theory, congruence is a more central concept than consistency.

T F Q4. Holland finds stereotyping of occupations by individuals to be useful in trying to make a career choice.

T F Q5. The inventory "My Vocational Situation" gives scores on each of the six Holland types.

T F Q6. Someone who works as a toll booth collector works in an environment that Holland would call undifferentiated.

T F Q7. Enterprising and Investigative types are inconsistent occupations.

T F Q8. Identity can be an important goal in career counseling.

T F Q9. Consistency can be an important goal in career counseling.

T F Q10. Investigating the relationship of various personality characteristics to Holland's personality types is an important area of research into Holland's theory.

47

Multiple choice items: Select the best answer from the alternatives given. Answer each question from the point of view of work adjustment theory.

Q11.   Which of the following is not one of Holland's six types of environments?

    a.   Altruism
    b.   Conventional
    c.   Investigative
    d.   Realistic

Q12.   According to Holland, an accountant is likely to prefer this type of work.

    a.   Artistic
    b.   Conventional
    c.   Enterprising
    d.   Investigative

Q13.   According to Holland, which types of people are likely to be found teaching in a high school?

    a.   Artistic
    b.   Enterprising
    c.   Investigative
    d.   Social

Q14.   Enjoying fixing radios and television sets would be associated with this Holland type.

    a.   Conventional
    b.   Enterprising
    c.   Investigative
    d.   Realistic

Q15.   Individuals who enjoy making real estate deals are likely to be found in this environment.

    a.   Artistic
    b.   Enterprising
    c.   Investigative
    d.   Social

Q16.   An individual who has an A I E personality type is likely to be found to prefer this environment.

    a.   A I E
    b.   E A I
    c.   R C S
    d.   S C R

Q17.   An assessment instrument that is used to measure personality type in Holland's theory is

    a.   the Minnesota Importance Questionnaire.
    b.   My Vocational Situation.
    c.   the Self Directed Search.
    d.   the Sixteen Personality Factors Questionnaire.

Q18. Pablo very much likes music and is considering being a musician. According to Holland, this match could best be described as

    a.   congruent.
    b.   consistent.
    c.   incongruent.
    d.   inconsistent.

Q19. Sandy enjoys music but very little else. According to Holland, her personality fits with this term.

    a.   congruent
    b.   consistent
    c.   differentiated
    d.   inconsistent

Q20. Lazlo has interests in financial management and sales management. These represent two Holland types that are

    a.   congruent.
    b.   consistent.
    c.   incongruent.
    d.   inconsistent.

Q21. The environment in an assembly line where people perform the same tasks all day can best be considered

    a.   congruent.
    b.   differentiated.
    c.   incongruent.
    d.   undifferentiated.

Q22. Which of the following Holland concepts does not make use of the six Holland types?

    a.   congruence
    b.   consistency
    c.   differentiation
    d.   identity

Q23. Holland's theory can be used

    a.   only with men.
    b.   only with women.
    c.   with adolescents and adults.
    d.   with children.

Q24.   Ozzie works in an automotive dealership where he and the other sales personnel enjoy their work and find that it fits them. Ozzie and his coworker are said to be _____ with their environment.

    a.   congruent
    b.   consistent
    c.   differentiated
    d.   identified

Q25.   Which of these terms best describes Holland's theory?

    a.   complex
    b.   disorganized
    c.   designed for middle school students rather than adults.
    d.   simple

ANSWER KEY

1.	b	11.	d	Q8.	T	Q18.	a
2.	b	12.	a	Q9.	F	Q19.	c
3.	b			Q10.	T	Q20.	b
4.	a	Q1.	T	Q11.	a	Q21.	b
5.	d	Q2.	F	Q12.	b	Q22.	d
6.	d	Q3.	T	Q13.	d	Q23.	c
7.	b	Q4.	T	Q14.	d	Q24.	a
8.	c	Q5.	F	Q15.	b	Q25.	d
9.	c	Q6.	F	Q16.	a		
10.	a	Q7.	T	Q17.	c		

CHAPTER 6
MYERS-BRIGGS TYPE THEORY

A theory of personality rather than a theory of career development

Perceiving and judging

    Perceiving

        Sensing

        Intuiting

    Judging

        Thinking

        Feeling

Combinations of perceiving and judging

    Sensing and thinking

    Sensing and feeling

    Intuition and feeling

    Intuition and thinking

The preference for perception or judgment

Extraversion and introversion

The 16 type combinations

Dominant and auxiliary processes

The role of occupational information

The role of assessment instruments

Applying the theory to women and culturally diverse populations

    Falsification of type

Counselor issues

    Extraversion

    Introversion

CHAPTER 6

MYERS-BRIGGS TYPE THEORY

EXERCISE 6.1

HOW DO YOU MAKE DECISIONS?

Part One

How Do You View Events and Circumstances in Your Life?

From the two boxes below, circle those characteristics that best fit you.

Box 1	Box 2
Present orientation	Future orientation
Following an orderly path in solving problems	Finding new ways to solve problems
Improving skills you have	Learning new skills
Working steadily	Working in energetic spurts
Understand in a step by step process	Reach an understanding quickly
Following routines	Avoiding routine
Don't care about being inspired	Rely on inspiration
Develop something new by adapting something else	Use personal insight to be creative

E. 1. List jobs or job tasks that fit with those characteristics that you have circled. List the characteristic then the job or job task.

_____

_____

_____

_____

Part Two

How Do You Make Judgments about Events in Your Life?

From the two boxes below, circle those characteristics that best fit you.

Box 3	Box 4
Putting things in order	Valuing harmony
Being logical and clear minded	Being sympathetic
Not revealing your emotions	Being aware of the feelings of others
Being treated fairly	Receiving praise and attention
Responding to thoughts of others	Responding to the feelings of others

E. 2. List jobs or job tasks that fit with those characteristics that you have circled. List the characteristic then the job or job task.

_____

_____

_____

Part Three

When You Make Decisions, Do You Pay More Attention to Viewing Events and Circumstances in Your Life or Making Judgments About Them?

From the two boxes below, circle those characteristics that best fit you.

Box 5 – Making Judgments	Box 6 – Viewing Events
Deal with new and different situations	Develop and follow a plan
Be open to alternatives	Finish tasks
Procrastinate about decisions	Make decisions quickly
Work on several projects at once	Stick to one project
Want to know more details before starting a new task	Learn the basics before starting a new task
Be open to changing your mind about a new decision	Be satisfied and want to move on when you make a new decision

53

E. 3. List jobs or job tasks that fit with those characteristics that you have circled. List the characteristic then the job or job task.

_____

_____

_____

Part Four

When You Make Decisions, Are You Influenced More By Your Own Inner Thoughts or by Concern About Other People and Outside Events?

From the two boxes below, circle those characteristics that best fit you.

Box 7 – About Others	Box 8 – Inner Thoughts
Being active	Thinking quietly
Like meeting people	Prefer to be on your own
Don't like to work alone for long periods of time	Like to work alone for long periods of time
Are interested in how people do a task	Are interested in the ideas behind a task
Quicker to act than to think	Quicker to think than to act
Prefer to work with people than alone	Prefer to work alone than with people

E. 4. List jobs or job tasks that fit with those characteristics that you have circled. List the characteristic then the job or job task.

_____

_____

Part Five

Summary

E. 5. How well do the characteristics, the jobs, and the job tasks that you have listed describe your personality and job preference? Explain.

_____

_____

54

E. 6. Describe your impression of this method of characterizing personality and work style preference.

_____

_____

_____

MATCH THE BOXES WITH THE EIGHT MYERS-BRIGGS TYPES

After you have read the chapter, match the names of the eight boxes below with the eight Myers-Briggs types.

1.	Box 1	a.	Sensing
2.	Box 2	b.	Intuiting
3.	Box 3	c.	Thinking
4.	Box 4	d.	Feeling
5.	Box 5	e.	Perception
6.	Box 6	f.	Judgment
7.	Box 7	g.	Extraversion
8.	Box 8	h.	Introversion

MYERS-BRIGGS TYPES IN CAREER CHOICE COUNSELING

The following example describes a client who is making a career choice. Information will be given to you so that you can choose what Myers-Briggs type is being described. This should help you become more familiar with the Myers-Briggs typology.

Ashley is a junior in college who is majoring in business. She does not know whether to pursue a career in sales, management, finance, or accounting. She is talking to you about her experience last summer when she worked as a receptionist in a real estate agency.

1. Ashley enjoyed answering the phones and making sure that the messages she gave were accurate. She prided herself on never making a mistake when she was writing down phone numbers. Her manager was impressed with Ashley's attention to detail. When she would report conversations that she had with clients in the office, she would present the details to her manager in a clear way. This description of Ashley fits this Myers-Briggs type.

   a.   Feeling
   b.   Intuition
   c.   Sensing
   d.   Thinking

2. After she had gathered data from clients about their schedules to meet with real estate agents, Ashley would be systematic in her analysis of the information and give a clear report to her boss. This description of Ashley fits this Myers-Briggs type.

    a.   Feeling
    b.   Intuition
    c.   Sensing
    d.   Thinking

3. Ashley's style of gathering information in her summer job is similar to the way she approaches preparing to take college exams. Although she pays attention to the specific details of her homework assignment, Ashley is most concerned with logically considering her decisions when she writes her answers to the problem. Which of these Myers-Briggs types is most significant in the way she approaches her decision-making?

    a.   Artistic
    b.   Conventional
    c.   Judging
    d.   Sensing

4. Ashley was friendly with her co-workers whom she worked with in her summer job. However, she very much enjoyed quiet times when she could think about problems at work as well as think about future plans. Sometimes it was an effort for her to be outgoing with her co-workers. Which of these Myers-Briggs types is most prominent in this description of Ashley?

    a.   Extraversion
    b.   Introversion
    c.   Judging
    d.   Perceiving

5. If Ashley's Myers-Briggs type is ISTJ, she is most likely to prefer the work of a(an)_____. (Hint: See Table 6-2 [p.167] of the text.)

    a.   accountant
    b.   counselor
    c.   musician
    d.   public relations worker

MYERS-BRIGGS TYPES IN WORK ADJUSTMENT COUNSELING

In this example, Tyrone is having difficulty working under the supervision of his boss, Brandon. Tyrone is in charge of the sporting goods department in a large department store. He reports directly to the assistant manager, Brandon. Brandon is frustrated by Tyrone's lack of attention to detail. Tyrone likes to think on a grand scale, whereas Brandon's style is to use standard methods to solve problems and to attend to detail.

6. Brandon most closely fits this Myers-Briggs type.

    a.   Feeling
    b.   Intuiting
    c.   Sensing
    d.   Thinking

7. Tyrone most closely fits this Myers-Briggs type.

    a.   Feeling
    b.   Intuiting
    c.   Sensing
    d.   Thinking

Brandon is frustrated by observing Tyrone taking time away from his department to consider new ways to plan to improve the department and to think about his professional goals. When Brandon was a department manager, he was often trying to help his employees improve their sales skills and concerned about helping his customers find merchandise that they were looking for.

8. Brandon most closely fits this Myers-Briggs type.

    a.   Extraversion
    b.   Introversion
    c.   Judging
    d.   Perceiving

9. Tyrone most closely fits this Myers-Briggs type.

    a.   Extraversion
    b.   Introversion
    c.   Judging
    d.   Perceiving

10. According to Myers-Briggs type theory, Brandon would be advised to try to

    a.   change his type to fit Tyrone's.
    b.   fire Tyrone.
    c.   get Tyrone to change his type
    d.   understand Tyrone's type.

11. If you were a counselor, helping Tyrone deal with his frustration with his boss, Brandon, you might point out that

    a.   being introverted is a good thing.
    b.   individuals may have a preference for type but use all types in their daily lives.
    c.   Myers-Briggs types are permanent and cannot change.
    d.   his Myers-Briggs type and Brandon's type are compatible in every possible way.

12. To help Tyrone better understand his frustration with Brandon's suggestion that he spend more time with customers and more time with his sales personnel, it might be helpful, from a Myers-Briggs perspective, to have Tyrone

      a.   examine his scores on the Minnesota Importance Questionnaire and discuss them with the counselor.
      b.   put more effort into improving his sales figures.
      c.   readjust his negative attitude towards Brandon.
      d.   take the Myers-Briggs Type Indicator and discuss the implications of it.

APPLYING MYERS-BRIGGS TYPE THEORY TO WOMEN AND CULTURALLY DIVERSE GROUPS

Does this theory have different implications for men and women? Explain.

_____

_____

_____

_____

_____

What implications does Myers-Briggs theory have for counseling people from diverse populations?

_____

_____

_____

_____

_____

_____

58

STRENGTHS AND LIMITATIONS

What do you see as the strengths and limitations of Myers-Briggs type theory?

Strengths	Limitations
_____	_____
_____	_____
_____	_____
_____	_____

MYERS-BRIGGS TYPE THEORY: A QUIZ

True or false items: Decide if the following items are more "true" or more "false" as they apply to concepts discussed in this chapter.

T   F   Q1.   Myers-Briggs type theory is a limited form of trait and factor theory.

T   F   Q2.   According to Myers-Briggs type theory, this would be a good definition of introversion: "Shy and does not like to interact with others."

T   F   Q3.   Myers-Briggs type theory can be used without other career development theories to help individuals make career choices.

T   F   Q4.   Perception and judgment are the overarching concepts used to understand Myers-Briggs type theory.

T   F   Q5.   The Myers-Briggs Type Indicator gives scores on each of the eight Myers-Briggs types.

T   F   Q6.   Individuals who like to think a lot before they act and are content to work alone may feel comfortable being described as introverted.

T   F   Q7.   According to Myers-Briggs type theory, thinking and feeling are two opposite ends of a continuum.

T   F   Q8.   According to Myers-Briggs type theory, sensing and perceiving are two opposite ends of a continuum.

T   F   Q9.   The goal of using Myers-Briggs type theory in career counseling is to define the type of person you are.

T   F   Q10.   The Myers-Briggs Type Indicator has been translated into many languages throughout the world.

Multiple choice items: Select the best answer from the alternatives given. Answer each question from the point of view of Myers-Briggs type theory.

Q11. Which of the following is not one of the Myers-Briggs types?

    a. Altruism
    b. Extraversion
    c. Perception
    d. Sensing

Q12. According to Myers-Briggs type theory, a credit manager is likely to prefer this type.

    a. Conventional
    b. Enterprising
    c. Intuitive
    d. Investigative

Q13. Sally is interested in the tasks she does as a graphic artist and enjoys learning about the tasks of others. She enjoys talking to many people that she works with about their work and their families. Sally is most likely to fit this Myers-Briggs type.

    a. Extraversion
    b. Introversion
    c. Intuitive
    d. Thinking

Q14. Marvin is very patient with routine detail in his work as a biologist. Friends are sometimes surprised by this, as he is extremely intelligent. This Myers-Briggs type most closely fits Marvin's tolerance for detail.

    a. Extraversion
    b. Intuition
    c. Judgment
    d. Sensing

Q15. Burt is very analytic in his decision making. He worries about whether or not his decision will be right, not how it will affect others. Burt's Myers-Briggs type would be

    a. Feeling.
    b. Extraversion.
    c. Sensing.
    d. Thinking.

Q16. In Myers-Briggs type theory,

    a. first one intuits, then one senses.
    b. first one becomes an extravert, then one becomes an introvert.
    c. first one perceives, then one judges.
    d. first one thinks, then one becomes an introvert.

Q17. Glenda has difficulty in her management job because she dislikes making decisions that might hurt people and then having to tell them. Glenda is most likely to fit this Myers-Briggs type.

    a.   Feeling
    b.   Extraversion
    c.   Sensing
    d.   Thinking

Q18. Melinda is upset at times with Barry as she would like to talk to him about things that go on at work, Barry tends to keep communication to a minimum. Melinda is most likely to fit this Myers-Briggs type.

    a.   Extraversion
    b.   Introversion
    c.   Sensing
    d.   Thinking

Q19. Barry finds Melinda to be intrusive and wishes she would leave him alone to ponder issues that he considers to be important. Barry would most likely fit this Myers-Briggs type.

    a.   Extroversion
    b.   Introversion
    c.   Sensing
    d.   Thinking

Q20. In counseling, Myers-Briggs type theory can best be used to

    a.   label individuals as specific Myers-Briggs types.
    b.   help individuals understand how they may fit into certain types of work environments.
    c.   make predictions about future satisfaction in specific work environments.
    d.   suggest careers someone should enter.

Q21. In counseling, it is helpful for counselors to understand how their own type fits with

    a.   the client's own type.
    b.   the career choice or work pressures that the client is experiencing.
    c.   the type of the client's significant other.
    d.   the type of the occupation that best fits the client.

Q22. In Myers-Briggs type theory, the dominant process provides a way for understanding

    a.   how an individual decides whom to take an authoritarian approach with.
    b.   what type an individual uses to dominate others.
    c.   when an individual is most likely to cause problems in counseling.
    d.   which type is the guiding one for an individual.

Q23.   In Myers-Briggs type theory, the auxiliary process provides a way for understanding

     a.   an individual's Myers-Briggs type in an easy to comprehend approach.
     b.   only the types of groups an individual chooses to join.
     c.   which type is the guiding one for an individual.
     d.   which type is the second most important one for an individual.

Q24.   When individuals are taught to respond in certain ways and keep their true type hidden, this process is referred to as

     a.   differentiation of type.
     b.   falsification of type.
     c.   identification of type.
     d.   sensitization of type.

Q25.   Myers-Briggs type theory was originally developed as a(an)

     a.   career development theory.
     b.   economic theory.
     c.   personality theory.
     d.   sociological theory.

ANSWER KEY

For the "Match the Boxes" exercise on page 55: Correct answers = 1a, 2b, 3c, 4d, 5e, 6f, 7g, 8h.

1. c	11. b	Q7. T	Q17. a
2. d	12. d	Q8. F	Q18. a
3. c		Q9. F	Q19. b
4. b		Q10. T	Q20. b
5. a	Q1. T	Q11. a	Q21. a
6. c	Q2. F	Q12. c	Q22. d
7. b	Q3. F	Q13. a	Q23. d
8. a	Q4. T	Q14. d	Q24. b
9. b	Q5. F	Q15. d	Q25. c
10. d	Q6. T	Q16. c	

CHAPTER 7
CAREER DEVELOPMENT IN CHILDHOOD

Career related issues that affect children until the age of 12

Super's model of the career development of children

    Curiosity

    Exploration

    Information

    Key figures

    Internal versus external control

    Development of interests

    Time perspective

    Self-concept and planfulness

Using Super's model in counseling children

    Types of elementary school guidance problems

    Typical family problems

Gottfredson' theory of self-creation, circumscription, and compromise

    Cognitive growth

    Self-creation

    Gender-drives-experience theory

    Internal compass

    Niches

Circumscription

    1. Orientation to size and power (3 to 5)

    2. Orientation to sex roles (6 to 8)

    3. Orientation to social valuation (9 to 13)

    4. Orientation to the internal unique self

    Compromise

Implications of Gottfredson's theory for Super's theory

Use of Gottfredson's and Super's concepts in counseling

Career development of children from culturally diverse backgrounds

The role of occupational information

    School to work programs for children

    Experiential career guidance model

The role of assessment instruments

Counselor issues

CHAPTER 7

CAREER DEVELOPMENT IN CHILDHOOD

EXERCISE 7.1

CAREER DEVELOPMENT IN CHILDHOOD (SUPER)

E. 1. When you were in kindergarten, first grade, and second grade what were you curious about? (Curiosity)

_____

_____

_____

E. 2. What did you would like to play with and explore? (Exploration)

_____

_____

E. 3. When you were in second and third grade, what did you like to learn inside school and outside of school? (Information)

_____

_____

_____

E. 4. When you were in second, third, and fourth grade, whom did you most admire (teachers, parents, relatives, athletes, movie stars)? What did you admire about them? (Key Figures)

_____

_____

_____

_____

E. 5. Try to remember an important incident or event that occurred between the ages of five and ten when you made a decision on your own rather than waiting to be told what to do. (Internal versus External Control)

_____

_____

_____

E. 6. Describe a time when you were able to develop a sense of how long it would take to achieve something that would take at least several weeks to accomplish. (Time Perspective)

_____

_____

_____

EXERCISE 7.2

CAREER DEVELOPMENT IN CHILDHOOD (GOTTFREDSON)

E. 7. How did you create yourself? How did certain experiences interact with biological factors such as writing ability, math ability, or other factors to form your occupational preferences? (Self-Creation)

_____

_____

_____

E. 8. Give two examples of how your career choices have been influenced by biological factors such as musical, artistic, or athletic ability.

_____

_____

_____

_____

65

E. 9. Describe your knowledge of occupations (your cognitive map of occupations) when you were 10 years old. Which occupations were prominent in the map and which ones were missing? (Cognitive Map)

_____

_____

_____

_____

E. 10. Give examples of two occupations that you eliminated from consideration (you were probably unaware of this) when you were in elementary school. Choose occupations that **did not fit** your gender or were not prestigious enough. How old were you and why did you give up on the occupations? (Circumscription)

_____

_____

_____

_____

E. 11. Give examples of two occupations that you decided were not for you when you were in elementary school. Choose occupations that **did not seem accessible** to you because of your gender or because your grades weren't good enough. How old were you and why did you give up on the occupations? (Compromise)

_____

_____

_____

_____

PLANNING CAREER DEVELOPMENT ACTIVITIES FOR CHILDREN USING SUPER'S THEORY

The following questions describe activities that would be appropriate for elementary school children. These activities describe a variety of purposes for activities that are consistent with Super's theory of childhood career development. You will be asked questions that relate to key concepts that form the basis of Super's theory.

1. You assist a fifth grade math teacher in finding an accountant to discuss how she uses math in her work and to describe what she does. You talk to the accountant so that she can help students explore math more so that they become more

   a.   curious.
   b.   focused on time perspective.
   c.   mature.
   d.   withdrawn.

2. If the accountant is very successful in describing what she does, she may become a

   a.   friend.
   b.   key figure.
   c.   parental surrogate.
   d.   role model.

3. All but one of these activities is appropriate behavior for children after having participated in the class room exercise with the accountant.

   a.   development of interests in math
   b.   exploring concepts that do not contain math
   c.   improving their own self-concept
   d.   withdrawing from exploring occupational information

4. Students who become distracted and have to be disciplined on a field trip to the accountant's firm may not have yet developed

   a.   external control.
   b.   information about accounting.
   c.   internal control.
   d.   time perspective.

5. Using Piaget's concepts of cognitive development within Super's theory, it would be helpful for the accountant to be careful to present material to fifth grader's that is not too
   a.   abstract.
   b.   boring.
   c.   exploratory.
   d.   planful.

6. According to Super, the ultimate purpose of childhood activities such as field trips to an accountant's office is to promote

   a.   curiosity.
   b.   development of interests.
   c.   self-concept.
   d.   time perspective.

CONCEPTUALIZING THE CAREER DEVELOPMENT OF CHILDREN USING AN EXAMPLE THAT APPLIES GOTTFREDSON'S THEORY

In this example, I will describe some examples of events in Carol's life. Carol has two brothers who are three and five years older than she is. Her mother works in food service at a high school cafeteria and her father is a dry wall installer. You will use Gottfredson's theory to label the nature of the event that she is going through.

7. According to Gottfredson, Carol's process of self-creation will occur as her social factors such as gender and prestige interact with _____ as she develops her view of her world and of occupations.

      a.   biological factors.
      b.   image norms.
      c.   her self-concept.
      d.   circumscription.

8. Because Carol grew up in Arizona near a desert, her cognitive map of occupations is less likely to include _____ occupations than if she grew up on the West Coast of the United States.

      a.   gender appropriate.
      b.   high status.
      c.   boating.
      d.   selling.

9. When Carol was four years old, she was impressed by the dry wall panels that her father would occasionally unload from his truck. At that time, she decided that when she grew up she would be a house builder. Carol could be described as being in which of these stages of circumscription? Orientation to

      a.   sex roles
      b.   size and power
      c.   social valuation
      d.   the internal unique self

10. When Carol was seven she decided that she wanted to be a teacher. She was very much impressed by Ms. Mitchell's good natured instructional methods that she used in her second grade class. She dropped her interest in construction of houses as she decided that it was a job for boys. Carol could be described as being in which of these stages of circumscription? Orientation to

      a.   sex roles
      b.   size and power
      c.   social valuation
      d.   the internal unique self

11. When Carol was 11 she decided that she would work in the local auto assembly plant. Her mother's mother and sister had worked there for years and had liked the union wages that they earned. None of Carol's family had gone to college and being a teacher seemed like a career that was not something that people like Carol did. Carol could be described as being in which of these stages of circumscription? Orientation to

    a.   sex roles
    b.   size and power
    c.   social valuation
    d.   the internal unique self

12. Carol is now 15 years old. She has been a very good student in school. She has done well in all subjects and has enjoyed being with students who like school. Carol has had a job in a drug store where she helped customers. She also has discussed managing a drug store with both the store manager and her assistant. They have been impressed with Carol's enthusiasm about her work. Carol is now considering going to college to study business. Carol could be described as being in which of these stages of circumscription? Orientation to

    a.   sex roles
    b.   size and power
    c.   social valuation
    d.   the internal unique self

13. According to Gottfredson, Carol, through her many experiences in and outside of school, is moving into her own

    a.   environment.
    b.   life role.
    c.   niche.
    d.   setting.

14. When Carol was 11 and had given up teaching as a possible occupation because no one in her family had done a job like that, she was, according to Gottfredson, considering an occupation that was

    a.   one her mother would not consider.
    b.   outside her tolerable level boundary.
    c.   outside her niche.
    d.   too difficult for her.

15. Carol, now 15, is considering accounting, management, social work, and being a park ranger. At this point, as she considers possible careers, she may need to _____ her choices due to financial circumstances.

    a.   circumscribe
    b.   compromise
    c.   limit
    d.   readjust

APPLYING SUPER'S AND GOTTFREDSON'S THEORY TO GIRLS AND CULTURALLY DIVERSE GROUPS

Does Super's theory have different implications for boys and girls? Explain.

_____

_____

_____

_____

_____

Does Gottfredson's theory have different implications for males and females? Explain.

_____

_____

_____

_____

_____

What implications does Super's theory have for counseling children from diverse populations?

_____

_____

_____

What implications does Gottfredson's theory have for counseling children from diverse populations?

_____

_____

_____

_____

STRENGTHS AND LIMITATIONS

What do you see as the strengths and limitations of Super's theory?

Strengths   Limitations

_____   _____

_____   _____

_____   _____

_____   _____

What do you see as the strengths and limitations of Gottfredson's theory?

Strengths   Limitations

_____   _____

_____   _____

_____   _____

_____   _____

CAREER DEVELOPMENT IN CHILDHOOD: A QUIZ

True or false items: Decide if the following items are more "true" or more "false" as they apply to concepts discussed in this chapter.

T   F   Q1.   According to Super, a major goal of children's career development is for children to eventually develop a sense of planfulness.

T   F   Q2.   From Super's point of view, career development starts in very young children as their curiosity leads to exploration.

T   F   Q3.   Super felt that children could make good career choices as early as the age of ten.

T   F   Q4.   According to Jean Piaget, achieving the period of formal operations would allow children to think abstractly about career choice.

T   F   Q5.   In Super's theory, it is children's peers rather than adults that are important in the career development of children.

T   F   Q6.   According to Gottfredson, biological factors become less important in career development as children grow older.

71

T F Q7. Gottfredson examines sociological factors in her theory more than Super does in his theory.

T F Q8. If June's choice not to become a rocket scientist is due to the influence of gender on her decision-making, then Gottfredson would refer to this process as circumscription.

T F Q9. According to Gottfredson, young children are attuned to social class from the age of four through adulthood.

T F Q10. Gottfredson's theory of career development in childhood specifies the influence of biological factors more than Super's does.

Multiple choice items: Select the best answer from the alternatives given. Answer each question from the point of view of childhood career development theory.

Q11. Even in infants, this concept basic to career development can be observed.

    a.   exploration
    b.   internal control
    c.   planfulness
    d.   time perspective

Q12. According to Super's theory, which of these would interfere with a child developing career maturity?

    a.   circumscription
    b.   key figures
    c.   time perspective
    d.   withdrawal

Q13. For Super, the goal of childhood career development is for children to develop both their self-concept and

    a.   exploration.
    b.   niches.
    c.   planfulness.
    d.   withdrawal.

Q14. According to Piaget, the ability to imagine career and other possibilities comes at this stage.

    a.   sensorimotor
    b.   preoperational
    c.   concrete operational
    d.   formal operational

Q15. Developing a sense of industriousness rather than a feeling of inferiority is an important task that should occur between the ages of six to eleven, according to

    a.   Erikson.
    b.   Gottfredson.
    c.   Piaget.
    d.   Super.

72

Q16. According to Super's theory, as children grow older they develop

    a.   external control.
    b.   internal control.
    c.   niches.
    d.   withdrawal.

Q17. In Super's theory of childhood career development, exploratory behavior leads to the acquisition of information that leads to the development of

    a.   conflict
    b.   curiosity.
    c.   interest.
    d.   withdrawal.

Q18. The child who cannot conceive of what it takes to go to college and graduate school to become a physical therapist, has yet to develop, according to Super,

    a.   curiosity.
    b.   internal control.
    c.   tolerable level boundaries.
    d.   time perspective.

Q19. According to Gottfredson, the internal genetic compass

    a.   determines children's occupational choices.
    b.   directs children to gender relevant choices.
    c.   determines the role of prestige in children's career choices.
    d.   is a guide to experiences children are likely to prefer.

Q20. Gottfredson's view of the role of biology in her theory of career development is that biological factors

    a.   become less important as one gets older.
    b.   become more important as one gets older.
    c.   biological are not as important as social factors.
    d.   are of little importance as environmental factors are extremely important after a child enters school.

Q21. Shanda is four years old. According to Gottfredson, she is most likely to be influenced in her occupational selection by her observations of

    a.   social niches.
    b.   learning about women's work by observing her mother.
    c.   objects like gardening tools.
    d.   the prestige level of occupations.

Q22. Tim has developed the idea that construction trades are only for men. According to Gottfredson, he has developed a

a. sexist attitude.
b. social niche.
c. tolerable–sex type boundary.
d. violation of nature nurture theory.

Q23. When Cory pays attention to how prestigious it is to be a lawyer, she would be in this Gottfredson stage.

a. orientation to size and power
b. orientation to sex role
c. orientation to social valuation
d. orientation to the internal unique self

Q24. Rina is now 16 and believes that she will never have enough financial support to become a veterinarian. Instead she will become a veterinary technician. Her decision could best be described by this Gottfredson concept.

a. circumscription
b. consistency
c. compromise
d. congruence

Q25. Which of the following is NOT an example of school to work for elementary school children?

a. crossword puzzles containing occupational terms
b. oral reports on occupations
c. field trips to visit people at work
d. choosing potential tracks for high school courses

ANSWER KEY

1.	a	11.	c	Q6.	F	Q16.	b
2.	b	12.	d	Q7.	T	Q17.	c
3.	d	13.	c	Q8.	T	Q18.	d
4.	c	14.	b	Q9.	F	Q19.	d
5.	a	15.	b	Q10.	T	Q20.	b
6.	c	Q1.	T	Q11.	a	Q21.	c
7.	a	Q2.	T	Q12.	d	Q22.	c
8.	c	Q3.	F	Q13.	c	Q23.	c
9.	b	Q4.	T	Q14.	c	Q24.	c
10.	a	Q5.	F	Q15.	a	Q25.	d

CHAPTER 8
ADOLESCENT CAREER DEVELOPMENT

Educational commitments to career choice are made during adolescence

Factors influencing adolescent career development

    Formal thought (Piaget)

    Identity and role confusion (Erikson)

Super's growth stage of adolescent career development

    Fantasy stage (up to 12)

        Development of interests (at about 10)

        Development of capacities (about 11 to 14)

        Development of values (different values emerge at different times)

        Transition to the crystallizing substage (about 17 to 18)

Super's career maturity concept

    Career planning

    Career exploration

    Decision making

    World-of-work information

    Knowledge of the preferred occupational group

    Realism (not tested)

    Career orientation total

Identity and context

    Based on Erikson, developed by Marcia and Vondracek

        Diffusion

        Moratorium

        Foreclosure

        Achievement

The role of occupational information

    Psychtalk

    Occtalk

The role of assessment

Gender issues in adolescence

Career development of adolescents from diverse cultural backgrounds

Counselor issues

CHAPTER 8

ADOLESCENT CAREER DEVELOPMENT

EXERCISE 8.1

CAREER DEVELOPMENT IN ADOLESCENCE (SUPER)

E. 1. Give an example of a fantasy occupation that you had before the age of six, such as astronaut, elephant, cowboy, rock, or singer.

_____

E. 2. Describe an example of when interests in activities or occupations affected your career choices (perhaps around the age of 11). (Development of Interests)

_____

_____

_____

E. 3. Describe an example of when your abilities in activities or occupational tasks affected your career choices, such as coming to the realization that you could not be a professional athlete or musician. (Development of Capacities)

_____

_____

_____

_____

E. 4. At what age did values become important to you in your career choice? _____

_____

E. 4a. Which values became important to you and why? (Development of Values)

_____

_____

_____

_____

EXERCISE 8.2

CAREER MATURITY (SUPER)

E. 5. Describe how you approached career planning in the ninth and tenth grades. How is that different from what you would do now? (Career Planning)

_____

_____

_____

_____

E. 6. In high school, how did you explore careers? What resources did you use, such as parents, friends, books, movies, or counselors? (Career Exploration)

_____

_____

_____

_____

E. 7. In high school, how did you make career decisions? (Who helped you? How tentative were the decisions?) (Decision Making)

_____

_____

_____

_____

E. 8. In high school, how did you learn about jobs and how people made career decisions? (World-of-work Information)

_____

_____

_____

_____

E. 9. Describe your knowledge of the occupations that you were making decisions about when you were in high school. (Knowledge of Preferred Occupational Group)

_____

_____

_____

_____

FOLLOWING CHANGES IN JERMAINE'S CAREER CHOICES AS HE GROWS UP (SUPER'S AND VONDRACEK'S THEORIES)

When Jermaine was nine, he wanted to be a jet pilot. He thought that this would be exciting and he could fly low to the ground, seeing all kinds of places and scare people. He thought it would be neat to wear a uniform.

1. If you were Jermaine's guidance counselor you might view Jermaine as being in Super's stage of

    a.   fantasy.
    b.   development of capacities.
    c.   development of interests.
    d.   development of values.

2. As Jermaine's counselor, you observe that as Jermaine talks to you, he doesn't have any clear ideas of what he wants to do. According to Vondracek, he would be in this identity status.

    a.   diffusion
    b.   moratorium
    c.   foreclosure
    d.   achievement

3. As Jermaine reaches the age of 12, he starts to explore biology because he enjoys learning about how plants grow. According to Super, Jermaine would be in this category.

    a.   fantasy
    b.   development of capacities
    c.   development of interests
    d.   development of values

4. Having completed his eighth grade year with an A in biology, Jermaine decides he will take advanced biology as well as the basic biology course in high school. He has a sense of mastery in that area of study. According to Super, Jermaine would be in this category.

    a.   development of capacities
    b.   development of interests
    c.   development of values
    d.   transition period

5. Jermaine is now in the tenth grade. He is completing his first high school biology course. As he has been taking the class, he has been learning about the opportunities to do microscopic research on cells and discover ways to study and possibly treat cancers. The opportunity to help others with health problems appeals to him. According to Super, Jermaine would be in this category.

    a.   development of capacities
    b.   development of interests
    c.   development of values
    d.   transition period

6. In the spring of his junior year, Jermaine starts to think about colleges and which ones he might be able to afford to go to. He is thinking that he may want to be a medical researcher. According to Super, Jermaine would be in this category

    a.   development of capacities
    b.   development of interests
    c.   development of values
    d.   transition period

7. Jermaine wants to talk to you about his idea to wait a year before going to college. He has an opportunity to work on a large medical research team as a lab assistant. This would enable him to explore various career options. Jermaine would be discussing which of these concepts, which are important in Vondracek's theory of identity in context?

    a.   diffusion
    b.   moratoruim
    c.   foreclosure
    d.   achievement

DEALING WITH MELISSA'S CAREER MATURITY

Melissa is a ninth grader in a rural school district outside of Bozeman, Montana. Her father and mother operate a café in their small town. Melissa has yet to travel outside of Montana, although she would like to do so. Music has been her main interest. She has taken piano lessons since she was five and sings in the junior choir at church. Like her parents, she is religious and much of her spare time is spent in youth groups connected with her church.

8. Melissa's parents are concerned about what she will do and have asked her to talk to you, her guidance counselor. They are concerned that Melissa seems to have no interest in talking to you about what she will do when she graduates high school or in talking to them or anyone else about this subject. According to Super, Melissa is not concerned with Super's concept of

    a.   career exploration.
    b.   career maintenance.
    c.   role salience.
    d.   world-of-work information.

9. When you do talk to Melissa, you become aware that she has not talked to anyone about courses she might take in high school. She also has not talked about or thought about extracurricular activities that she might do next year and doesn't seem to care. The idea of working part time after school has not yet occurred to her, nor does she want to look at this issue. As her counselor, you are concerned that Melissa has not yet addressed this concept, which is a part of Super's model of career maturity. Melissa agrees that she hasn't done much in this area.

   a.   career exploration
   b.   career planning
   c.   decision making
   d.   world-of-work information

10. When you ask Melissa how she is going to decide what she will study or work in after school, she replies: "I don't have a clue." This suggests that she does not have knowledge about the following area of Super's model of career maturity.

   a.   career exploration
   b.   career planning
   c.   decision making
   d.   world-of-work information

11. As Melissa's counselor, you are concerned about her knowledge of career decision making and are likely to suggest

   a.   that she do some volunteer work.
   b.   that she spend more time with her music.
   c.   ways that she might learn how career decisions are made.
   d.   occupational information that she might learn.

12. When you ask Melissa what she knows about occupations that people in her community do, you are asking about this concept of Super's model of career maturity.

   a.   career exploration
   b.   decision making
   c.   vocational identity
   d.   world-of-work information

13. If you ask Melissa which one of 20 occupational groups she prefers, she is likely to reply,

   a.   "astronaut."
   b.   "huh?"
   c.   "physicist."
   d.   "park ranger."

14. Being unable to identify a group of preferred occupational groups from a list of 20 and describe them would indicate that Melissa has little knowledge in this area of Super's model of career maturity.

   a.   career exploration
   b.   decision making
   c.   knowledge of the preferred occupation
   d.   world-of-work information

15. Super refers to the general area that you have been discussing with Melissa as

    a.   career exploration.
    b.   career development attitudes.
    c.   career orientation.
    d.   decision making.

APPLYING SUPER'S THEORY TO ADOLESCENT GIRLS AND CULTURALLY DIVERSE GROUPS

Does Super's theory have different implications for adolescent boys and girls? Explain.

_____

_____

_____

_____

_____

What implications does Super's theory have for counseling adolescents from diverse populations?

_____

_____

_____

_____

STRENGTHS AND LIMITATIONS

What do you see as the strengths and limitations of Super's theory?

        Strengths   Limitations

Strengths	Limitations
_____	_____
_____	_____
_____	_____
_____	_____

81

What do you see as the strengths and limitations of Vondracek's theory?

Strengths   Limitations

_____   _____

_____   _____

_____   _____

_____   _____

CAREER DEVELOPMENT IN ADOLESCENCE: A QUIZ

True or false items: Decide if the following items are more "true" or more "false" as they apply to concepts discussed in this chapter.

T   F   Q1.   According to Super, a major goal of adolescent career development is for adolescents to develop a sense of fantasy.

T   F   Q2.   From Super's point of view, career maturity is important before helpful career decision making can take place.

T   F   Q3.   Vondracek believes that the achievement status is the goal of vocational identity.

T   F   Q4.   According to Super and his colleagues, the transition to the crystallization substage occurs late in high school and is the time that important decisions are made.

T   F   Q5.   According to Super, having information about the world-of-work is important before a student has attained career maturity.

T   F   Q6.   Super was concerned that adolescents would choose (foreclose on) an occupation without knowing what they want to do.

T   F   Q7.   Vondracek expanded on Erikson's theory of identity by focusing on the trust-mistrust stage.

T   F   Q8.   According to Marcia, going to a lecture series on occupational information would be an example of a moratorium.

T   F   Q9.   Becoming a lawyer because your mother says that would be a good occupation for you would be an example of being in Marcia's foreclosure stage.

T   F   Q10. Super's model of career maturity and Vondracek's model of identity and context are two different ways of viewing career development in adolescence.

Multiple choice items: Select the best answer from the alternatives given. Answer each question from the point of view of career development theory in adolescence.

Q11. According to Super, your interest in a school subject probably developed before your ability to judge your

    a.   decision making.
    b.   identity.
    c.   moratorium.
    d.   capacities or abilities.

Q12. According to Super, which ordering of childhood career development periods would be correct?

    a.   capacities, interests, fantasies
    b.   capacities, fantasies, interests
    c.   fantasies, interests, capacities
    d.   interests, fantasies, capacities

Q13. According to Super and his colleagues, assessing one's own abilities is necessary before one can

    a.   develop a sense of identity.
    b.   become vocationally mature.
    c.   enter the foreclosure stage.
    d.   experience job satisfaction.

Q14. According to Super's view of career maturity, a positive attitude towards _____ is important.

    a.   career exploration
    b.   circumscription
    c.   career identity
    d.   formal operations

Q15. According to Super's view of career maturity, Placido should have a good knowledge of _____ before he can be considered vocationally mature.

    a.   career decision making
    b.   career identity
    c.   diffusion
    d.   work adjustment

Q16. According to Super's view of career maturity, this concept is important when adolescents are about ready to make career choices.

    a.   achievement
    b.   diffusion
    c.   identity
    d.   realism

Q17. According to Super's view of career maturity, adolescents should have knowledge of _____ before making career decisions.

    a. capacities, interests, and values
    b. achievement, diffusion, and moratorium
    c. career planning, career exploration, decision making, and the world-of-work
    d. circumscription and compromise

Q18. According to Super's view of career maturity, Maria's knowledge of accounting, a field she is considering entering, would be called

    a. career exploration.
    b. career planning.
    c. knowledge of preferred occupational group.
    d. world-of-work information.

Q19. Whereas Super focuses on the adolescent's career development, Vondracek focuses on this but also the environment in which this occurs. This focus is called

    a. compromise.
    b. career maturity theory.
    c. developmental-contextual theory.
    d. socialization theory.

Q20. Maggie says to herself, "I could be a chemist." Super and his colleagues would call this

    a. backtalk.
    b. chalktalk.
    c. occtalk.
    d. psychtalk

Q21. Rick has decided to take a year off from college to learn more about himself and what he wants to do in the future. According to Marcia, this plan could be called

    a. a moratorium.
    b. achievement.
    c. diffusion.
    d. foreclosure.

Q22. Reba has a clear idea of what she wants to do and her career plans. According to Marcia, this identity status could best be called

    a. a moratorium.
    b. achievement.
    c. diffusion.
    d. foreclosure.

Q23.   World-of-work information is associated with this theorist.

a.   Erikson
b.   Holland
c.   Super
d.   Vondracek

Q24.   "Homer is developing a sense of vocational identity." This statement would most likely be made
by a counselor using this theory.

a.   Gottfredson's
b.   Holland's
c.   Super's
d.   Vondracek's

Q25.   Which of the following is NOT an example of research on vocational maturity?

a.   studying gender differences in vocational maturity scores
b.   studying differences in vocational maturity scores among adolescents of different cultures
c.   examining the vocational realism of adolescents by gender
d.   examining differences in the types of moratoriums depending on gender

ANSWER KEY

1.	a	11.	c	Q6.	F	Q16.	d
2.	a	12.	d	Q7.	F	Q17.	c
3.	c	13.	b	Q8.	F	Q18.	c
4.	a	14.	c	Q9.	T	Q19.	c
5.	c	15.	c	Q10.	T	Q20.	c
6.	d	Q1.	F	Q11.	d	Q21.	a
7.	b	Q2.	T	Q12.	c	Q22.	b
8.	a	Q3.	T	Q13.	b	Q23.	c
9.	b	Q4.	T	Q14.	a	Q24.	d
10.	c	Q5.	T	Q15.	a	Q25.	d

85

CHAPTER 9
LATE ADOLESCENT AND CAREER DEVELOPMENT

Role salience
 Differences in the importance of work to
  different people
 Importance of work depends on life
  stage

Life roles (Salience Inventory)
 Studying
 Working
 Community service
 Home and family
 Leisure activities
   Liptak's leisure theory of career
    development

Indicators of the salience of life roles (Salience
Inventory)
 Knowledge
 Commitment
 Participation
 Values expectations
   Ability utilization
   Achievement
   Aesthetics
   Altruism
   Autonomy
   Creativity
   Economic rewards
   Lifestyle
   Physical activity
   Prestige
   Risk
   Social interaction
   Variety
   Working conditions
   Aesthetics

Adult life stages
 [Maxicycle]
 [Minicycle]

 Exploration
   Crystallizing
   Specifying
   Implementing

Establishment
 Stabilizing
 Consolidating
 Advancing

Maintenance
 Holding
 Updating
 Innovating

Disengagement
 Decelerating
 Retirement planning
 Retirement living

[Recycling]

Super's life stages for women

 Stable homemaking career pattern
 Conventional career pattern
 Stable working career pattern
 Double-track career pattern
 Interrupted career pattern
 Unstable career pattern
 Multiple-trial career pattern

Bardwick's stages

 30 to 40 — women with children do not
 want to delay their career, they try to
 balance their professional role
 40 to 50 — more autonomy, more
 independent
 Over 50 — career accomplishments

Life stages of culturally diverse adults

 Conformity
 Dissonance
 Resistance and immersion
 Introspection
 Synergetic articulation and awareness

Counselor issues

CHAPTER 9

LATE ADOLESCENT AND ADULT CAREER DEVELOPMENT

EXERCISE 9.1

LIFE ROLES

E. 1. This exercise will help you determine which life roles are most important to you (Super's Role Salience)

What percent of your time in the last month have you spent in each of these activities? (Participation)	With "1" being the most important, rank your commitment to each of these roles. (Commitment)	Give a letter grade (A, B, C, D, or F) to indicate how much you know about each role. (Knowledge)
___ Studying	___ Studying	___ Studying
___ Working	___ Working	___ Working
___ Community Service	___ Community Service	___ Community Service
___ Home and Family	___ Home and Family	___ Home and Family
___ Leisure Activities	___ Leisure Activities	___ Leisure Activities

E. 2. List the role that you participate in most and explain why you do so. Also, explain how your participation in the role affects your participation in other roles. (Participation)

_____

_____

_____

_____

_____

E. 3. List the role that you feel is most important to you. Explain why it is more important than other roles. (Commitment)

_____

_____

_____

_____

E. 4. List the role that you know most about. Why do you know most about this role? What do you want to learn about other roles? (Knowledge)

_____

_____

_____

_____

E. 5. In what ways are your participation in, commitment to, and knowledge of roles that are important to you consistent or inconsistent? (For example, do you participate most in the role that you are most committed to?)

_____

_____

_____

_____

WORKING DURING YOUR LIFE SPAN

E. 6. What major tasks or activities do you expect to do in your lifetime? Depending on your current age, write in the spaces below what you did do, what you are doing, or what you will do. In doing this, describe work issues that you confronted, are confronting now, or might confront. (Adult Life Stages)

18 to 25 (Exploration)

_____

_____

26 to 45 (Establishment)

_____

_____

45 to 65 (Maintenance)

_____

_____

66 to ? (Disengagement)

_____

_____

E. 7. How do you see your work life changing as you age?

_____

_____

_____

_____

E. 8. In what ways are you likely to view work differently as you get older?

_____

_____

_____

_____

E. 9. Do you think you will be doing similar work in twenty years to what you are doing now (or studying to do)? Explain.

_____

_____

_____

_____

89

TANYA'S LIFE ROLES: AN EXAMPLE

Tanya just received her Master's of Business Administration four months ago. When she was doing her undergraduate work, she majored in sociology. After she graduated with that degree, she worked in the claims adjusting department of a large insurance firm. After one year of working in the claims adjusting department, Tanya was concerned that she would not be able to advance in the field. Although she continued to work a 40-hour week and some overtime, she started to plan to attend graduate school so she could get into management in human resources or some other area of business. She continued to do her work well, but lost some of her initial interest and enthusiasm. She looked forward to returning to school and learning new information about business.

She has just started a job as an assistant manager in the benefits office of a very large food company. She is pleased that she will have more independence than before and will be able to get a sense of achievement as she helps her company develop a benefit plan for a small company that it is forming which deals with a new product line.

1. When Tanya was employed in the claims adjusting department, she participated in this life role.

    a. community service
    b. leisure activities
    c. studying
    d. working

2. During the last year as a claims adjuster, Tanya was committed to this life role.

    a. community service
    b. leisure activities
    c. studying
    d. working

3. When Tanya worked as a claims adjuster and then went to graduate school, this indicator of the salience of life roles continually increased.

    a. commitment
    b. knowledge
    c. leisure activities
    d. value expectations

4. Tanya's desire to produce good results and to continue to set high goals for herself as well as to work independently are indicators of the importance of this life role.

    a. commitment
    b. knowledge
    c. participation
    d. values expectation

5. Tanya has spent as much time in her new job as her old one. Her change in this indicator of the importance of the working life role seems to stand out in her new job.

    a.   commitment
    b.   knowledge
    c.   participation
    d.   values expectation

6. Now that Tanya is working in her new job and no longer at graduate school, her participation and commitment to this life role have decreased significantly.

    a.   community service
    b.   leisure activities
    c.   studying
    d.   working

OBSERVATIONS ABOUT TANYA'S CAREER DEVELOPMENT

The following questions will ask you to identify which of Super's life stage is applicable to Tanya.

7. When Tanya is in graduate school and clarifying what type of work she is going to do, she is in this substage of Super's exploration stage.

    a.   crystallizing
    b.   holding
    c.   implementing
    d.   specifying

8. Just before Tanya graduates with her MBA, she is likely to be in this substage of Super's exploration phase.

    a.   crystallizing
    b.   holding
    c.   implementing
    d.   specifying

9. After Tanya has worked for the benefits department of the food company and starts to feel secure in the job, she is likely to be in which one of Super's stages?

    a.   exploration
    b.   establishment
    c.   maintenance
    d.   disengagement

10. Tanya has now been in the company for five years and would like to have more responsibility in her work. She is likely to be in which of these substages?

    a.   advancing
    b.   crystallizing
    c.   consolidating
    d.   stabilizing

11. The substage of Super's theory that Tanya is likely to be in after she becomes the manager of employee retirement benefits at age 51 is

    a.   innovating .
    b.   implementing.
    c.   stabilizing.
    d.   specifying.

12. When Tanya is 53 years old, a friend offers her the opportunity to be a partner in a real estate agency. The friend is well aware of Tanya's persuasive and organizational skills. Tanya prefers to stay in her current job. Tanya is likely to be in this stage of Super's adult development model.

    a.   exploration
    b.   establishment
    c.   maintenance
    d.   disengagement

13. This process of rethinking one's career plan is referred to as _____ by Super.

    a.   advancing
    b.   consolidating
    c.   recycling
    d.   updating

14. Bardwick would take a different view of Tanya's stage of career development when she is at the age of 53. Bardwick would see Tanya as being not in the maintenance stage, but in a stage of

    a.   balancing career and family.
    b.   career accomplishment.
    c.   disengagement.
    d.   stabilizing.

15. As an African American woman, Tanya has developed a mature sense of identity in terms described by Atkinson, Morten, and Sue. This has enabled her to deal with a few issues dealing with racial discrimination in ways that helped her feel good about her ability to handle such difficult situations. She is likely to be in this stage of Atkinson, Morten, and Sue's minority identity development model.

    a.   conformity
    b.   dissonance
    c.   resistance and immersion
    d.   synergetic articulation and awareness

APPLYING THEORIES TO WOMEN AND CULTURALLY DIVERSE GROUPS

What different implications does Super's theory have for men and women?

_____

_____

_____

_____

_____

What different implications does Bardwick's theory have for men and women?

_____

_____

_____

_____

_____

What implications does Atkinson, Morten, and Sue's theory have for counseling adults from diverse populations?

_____

_____

_____

_____

_____

What implications does Super's theory have for counseling adults from diverse populations?

_____

_____

_____

_____

_____

93

STRENGTHS AND LIMITATIONS

What do you see as the strengths and limitations of Super's adult development theory?

Strengths	Limitations
_____	_____
_____	_____
_____	_____
_____	_____
_____	_____

CAREER DEVELOPMENT IN LATE ADOLESCENCE AND ADULTHOOD: A QUIZ

True or false items: Decide if the following items are more "true" or more "false" as they apply to concepts discussed in this chapter.

T   F   Q1.   According to Super, a major goal of adult career development is for adults to decelerate and relax.

T   F   Q2.   From Super's point of view, it is not sufficient to examine the role of work for adults; one should examine other life roles as well.

T   F   Q3.   Fantasizing is one of the important adult life roles that Super believes is important.

T   F   Q4.   The expectation that various roles (values expectations) should meet a variety of value needs is an indicator of the salience of life roles, according to Super.

T   F   Q5.   Participation and intuition are two indicators of the importance of life roles, according to Super.

T   F   Q6.   According to Super, autonomy and working conditions are examples of values expectations.

T   F   Q7.   According to Super, crystallizing a career choice and specifying career preferences are substages of the exploration stage for adults.

T   F   Q8.   According to Super, one should first establish a career prior to entering the exploration stage.

T   F   Q9.   According to Super, individuals who move from one substage to the next one can be said to recycle into the next stage.

T   F   Q10. Bardwick's stages for women are almost identical to the stages proposed by Super.

Multiple choice items: Select the best answer from the alternatives given. Answer each question from the point of view of career development theory in adolescence.

Q11.   According to Super, your interest in a school subject could be described by Super as

    a.   commitment to the life role of studying.
    b.   knowledge of the life role of studying.
    c.   your commitment to the life role of home and family.
    d.   participation in the life role of home and family.

Q12.   According to Super, which of these is not an indicator of the importance of life roles?

    a.   commitment
    b.   creativity
    c.   participation
    d.   values expectations

Q13.   Still living with her mother, Kim, now 34, participates in collecting bugs, a childhood hobby. According to Super, she participates in this life role.

    a.   community service
    b.   home and family
    c.   leisure activities
    d.   working

Q14.   According to Super, which of the following would not be a value expectation?

    a.   achievement
    b.   aesthetics
    c.   career identity
    d.   risk

Q15.   Bart has just started his job as an insurance sales person. According to Super, Bart is likely to be in this substage.

    a.   crystallizing
    b.   holding
    c.   stabilizing
    d.   withdrawal

Q16.   Mavis has been working as a physician in a small group practice for 32 years. At the age of 66, she wants to cut back her hours to 20 hours a week. According to Super's view of adult career development, what substage would Mavis be in?

    a.   crystallizing
    b.   consolidating
    c.   decelerating
    d.   holding

Q17. Gunther is in his junior year in college. He is starting his second year of work for his college newspaper. During his sophomore year it became clearer to him that print journalism was a field he wanted to go into after graduation. According to Super, Gunther is in this substage.

    a.   crystallizing
    b.   consolidating
    c.   holding
    d.   innovating

Q18. One of these events is not addressed directly in Super's theory of adult career development.

    a.   starting a job
    b.   job promotion
    c.   racial discrimination
    d.   retirement

Q19. Yorena has been a registered nurse for ten years. After careful thinking, Yorena has decided to sell used cars at an automobile dealership in town. According to Super, she is in the process of

    a.   decelerating.
    b.   implementing.
    c.   recycling.
    d.   specifying.

Q20. When one is in the process of recycling, Super's theory states that one is likely to return to this substage.

    a.   crystallizing
    b.   consolidating
    c.   decelerating
    d.   stabilizing

Q21. Which of the following is not one of Super's career patterns for women?

    a.   balancing feminine and professional roles
    b.   double track career
    c.   interrupted
    d.   unstable

Q22. According to Bardwick, women over the age of 50 are likely to experience

    a.   career accomplishments.
    b.   depression.
    c.   recycling.
    d.   the maintenance stage.

Q23.   Atkinson, Morten, and Sue's minority development model examines

      a.   attitudes towards self.
      b.   attitudes towards work.
      c.   reports of discrimination.
      d.   recycling experiences.

Q24.   Questioning one's own minority culture can make it difficult to

      a.   assess one's own abilities, interests, and values.
      b.   experience racial discrimination.
      c.   recycle through Super's stages.
      d.   get a job.

Q25.   According to Super, which of the following is not an example of an adult career development substage?

      a.   crystallizing
      b.   internal-external control
      c.   specifying
      d.   updating

ANSWER KEY

1.	d	11.	a	Q6.	T	Q16.	c
2.	c	12.	c	Q7.	T	Q17.	a
3.	b	13.	c	Q8.	F	Q18.	c
4.	a	14.	b	Q9.	F	Q19.	c
5.	a	15.	d	Q10.	F	Q20.	a
6.	c	Q1.	F	Q11.	a	Q21.	a
7.	a	Q2.	T	Q12.	b	Q22.	a
8.	c	Q3.	F	Q13.	c	Q23.	a
9.	b	Q4.	T	Q14.	c	Q24.	a
10.	a	Q5.	F	Q15.	c	Q25.	b

CHAPTER 10
ADULT CAREER CRISES AND TRANSITIONS

Definitions of transitions and crises

Schlossberg's four types of transitions

    Anticipated
    Unanticipated
    Chronic hassles
    Nonevents

Hopson and Adams classification of transitions

    Voluntary
    Involuntary

Categories of career transitions

    Normative role transitions
    Anticipated and voluntary
    Occurs in Super's Exploration stage
    Become crises when not anticipated

Louis's five categories of normative transitions

    Entering or reentering the labor pool
    Taking on a different role in an organization
    Moving from one organization to another
    Changing professions
    Leaving the labor pool

Types of careers

    Boundaryless

    Protean

Career Transitions Inventory

    Readiness
    Confidence
    Control
    Perceived support
    Decision independence

Nonnormative career events

Persistent occupational problems

Hopson and Adams's model of adult transitions

Immobilization
Minimization
Self-doubt
Letting go
Testing out
Search for meaning
Internalization

Career crises affecting women

Temporary re-entry into and leave-taking from the labor force
Sexual harassment
Tills's five levels of sexual harassment

    1. Gender harassment
    2. Seductive behavior
    3. Sexual bribery
    4. Sexual coercion
    5. Sexual assault

Victim response to sexual harassment

    Internally focused strategies
    Externally focused strategies

Gutek and Koss's four stages of reacting to sexual harassment

    Confusion and self blame
    Fear and anxiety
    Depression and anxiety
    Disillusionment

Career crises affecting culturally diverse populations

    Discrimination
    Atkinson, Morten, and Sue's model

Counselor issues

CHAPTER 10

ADULT CAREER CRISES AND TRANSITIONS

EXERCISE 10.1

SCHOOL AND WORK EVENTS: CRISES AND TRANSITIONS

E. 1. How did you adjust and react to the following transitions and events?

E. 1a. Changing from middle school to high school.

_____

_____

_____

E. 1b. Taking your first paid job.

_____

_____

_____

E. 1c. Taking your first semester of college courses.

_____

_____

_____

E. 1d. Committing to a career choice.

_____

_____

_____

E. 1e. Moving away from home (even if temporary).

_____

_____

EXERCISE 10.2

REACTING TO A CAREER CRISIS

E. 2. Give an example of how you (or someone you know) reacted to a career crisis. Examples of situations include being fired, being laid off, being discriminated against at work, and being sexually harassed.

_____

_____

_____

_____

_____

E. 3. How did your (or someone you know) reaction to the event change over time? For example, what was the reaction the first day? What was the reaction a month later?

_____

_____

_____

_____

_____

GINA'S EMPLOYER GOES OUT OF BUSINESS: AN EXAMPLE (HOPSON AND ADAMS'S CRISIS THEORY)

Gina has been employed as a computer programmer for a software development company for six years. She is a single mother with a four-year-old daughter and a six-year-old son who lives outside of Richmond, Virginia. Her mother has been helping with childcare, but Gina has been the sole support for the family. The children's fathers have not contributed to the support of their children. Gina's company has lost several large contracts to competitors and must close. She was given one weeks notice to finish her assignments and to leave. The company is offering two weeks severance pay, but no help in finding a job.

1. When Gina's supervisor told her that the company was closing, she had no idea that this was going to happen. She had just moved to a more expensive apartment and was not prepared to finance the apartment from her savings. This type of transition has been referred to by Schlossberg as

    a. anticipated.
    b. a chronic hassle.
    c. an event that does not happened.
    d. unanticipated.

2. Hopson and Adams might refer to this event as

    a. anticipated and voluntary.
    b. unanticipated and voluntary.
    c. anticipated and involuntary.
    d. unanticipated and involuntary.

3. When Gina first heard the news that her job was to be eliminated, she had no thought that this would happen. According to Hopson and Adams, she is likely to experience this reaction to hearing about losing her job.

    a. immobilization
    b. letting go
    c. minimization
    d. self doubt

4. When Gina calls her mother to tell her what has happened, she does not panic and tries to reassure her mother that the company may change its mind about closing. This is a hope that Gina has come to believe. Her supervisor has not mentioned this to her. According to Hopson and Adams, she is likely to go through this stage.

    a. immobilization
    b. minimization
    c. letting go
    d. testing out

5. According to Hopson and Adams, Gina is most likely to experience this reaction a few days after the call to her mother.

    a. elation
    b. a feeling that she can master the situation and get a new job
    c. doubt that she can take care of her children by getting a new job
    d. an identity crisis

6. After another week has passed, Gina starts to think about how she will provide for her children, what temporary or other job she can get, and if any of her previous employers can help. According to Hopson and Adams, she is likely to experience this reaction.

    a. immobilization
    b. letting go
    c. self-doubt
    d. testing out

7. After Gina has been out of work for a month, she is able to make contacts with both new potential employers and previous employers. She has four job interviews lined up for the coming week. According to Hopson and Adams, she is likely to experience this reaction.

    a.   letting go
    b.   minimization
    c.   self-doubt
    d.   testing out

8. After Gina has been out of work for two months, she was able to get a temporary job as a programmer with no benefits, but a high hourly wage. In the process of doing so, she has developed new job seeking skills and a sense of being able to deal with unanticipated crises. According to Hopson and Adams, she is likely to experience this reaction.

    a.   letting go
    b.   minimization
    c.   internalization
    d.   testing out

JOB DISCRIMINATION AND SEXUAL HARASSMENT: AN EXAMPLE

Juanita is a 25-year-old woman who moved from Mexico two years ago to the United States. She has taken a job in a furniture plant, where she helps to finish wooden parts for inexpensive tables. In this job, she has experienced several examples of discrimination. Her supervisor, Alvin, is a Caucasian man who appears both bored and critical.

9. Alvin has touched Juanita inappropriately several times as she was leaning over her workbench. Juanita is upset and ashamed. Alvin's behavior would be considered _____ sexual harassment.

    a.   low level
    b.   moderate level
    c.   high level
    d.   not meeting the criteria for

10. Because Juanita is both Mexican and a woman, she can be said to be someone who could experience

    a.   double jeopardy.
    b.   jeopardy.
    c.   self-doubt.
    d.   testing out.

11. According to Gutek and Koss, Juanita is most likely to feel _____ after the first time she has been sexually harassed.

    a.   a growth in coping skills
    b.   a sense of balance
    c.   confusion or self blame
    d.   disillusionment

12. According to Gutek and Koss, Juanita may experience

    a.   career maturity.
    b.   a moratorium.
    c.   a lack of support from her employer.
    d.   an identity crisis.

13. According to Gutek and Koss, when Juanita recognizes that the harassment is not her fault, she may become depressed or

    a.   angry.
    b.   elated.
    c.   involved in a search for meaning.
    d.   experience manic episodes.

14. Hopson and Adams see the eventual outcome of a crisis differently than Gutek and Koss. In their view of the outcome of a sexual harassment situation, Hopson and Adams would predict that Juanita would likely experience _____ as the sexual harassment crisis is resolved.

    a.   despair
    b.   disillusionment
    c.   internalization
    d.   self-blame

15. Hopson and Adams see the eventual outcome of a crisis differently than Gutek and Koss. In their view of the outcome of a sexual harassment situation, Gutek and Koss would predict that Juanita would likely experience _____ as the sexual harassment crisis is resolved.

    a.   despair
    b.   disillusionment
    c.   internalization
    d.   self-blame

APPLYING CRISIS THEORY TO ADULT MEN AND WOMEN

Does Hopson and Adams's theory have different implications for adult men and women? Explain.

_____

_____

_____

_____

_____

_____

103

How do Gutek and Koss's stages of reaction to sexual harassment experience have different implications for men and women? Explain.

_____

_____

_____

_____

_____

What implications does Hopson and Adam's theory have for counseling men and women from diverse populations?

_____

_____

_____

_____

What implications do Gutek and Koss's stages of reaction to sexual harassment have for counseling men and women from diverse populations?

_____

_____

_____

_____

STRENGTHS AND LIMITATIONS

What do you see as the strengths and limitations of Hopson and Adam's crisis theory?

Strengths   Limitations

_____   _____

_____   _____

_____   _____

_____   _____

104

What do you see as the strengths and limitations of Gutek and Koss's stages of reactions to sexual harassment?

Strengths   Limitations

_____   _____

_____   _____

_____   _____

_____   _____

_____   _____

ADULT CAREER CRISES AND TRANSITIONS: A QUIZ

True or false items: Decide if the following items are more "true" or more "false" as they apply to concepts discussed in this chapter.

T   F   Q1.   When a student graduates from high school, this transition can be called a chronic hassle.

T   F   Q2.   Ervin has been waiting for two years for a pay raise and has never received one. This transition can be called a nonevent.

T   F   Q3.   All unanticipated events can be assumed to be involuntary.

T   F   Q4.   According to Louis, moving from one employer to another can be considered a normative transition.

T   F   Q5.   One role of outplacement counselors is to help their clients deal with the emotional trauma of losing a job.

T   F   Q6.   According to Hopson and Adams, the first reaction that individuals are likely to have to a major career disruption is shock.

T   F   Q7.   According to Hopson and Adams, when individuals are laid off, they rarely doubt themselves, but are able to easily start to look for a new job.

T   F   Q8.   According to Hopson and Adams, the internalization stage is a positive one, in which individuals may develop coping skills and be enriched in many ways.

T   F   Q9.   Being self-directed in managing one's own career is a characteristic of a *protean* career.

T   F   Q10. According to Gutek and Koss, when women are sexually harassed, they are able to assert themselves and get support in the work place so that such events do not reoccur to them.

Multiple choice items: Select the best answer from the alternatives given. Answer each question from the point of view of theories of adult career crises and transitions.

Q11.　Which of the following is not a common career transition?

    a.　anticipated
    b.　chronic hassles
    c.　risk taking
    d.　unanticipated

Q12.　Deciding to go back to school after working for a year would be an example of this type of transition.

    a.　advancing
    b.　chronic hassle
    c.　involuntary
    d.　voluntary

Q13.　According to Louis, which of the following would NOT be an example of a normative transition?

    a.　crystallizing a career choice
    b.　entering the labor pool
    c.　moving from one organization to another
    d.　taking on a new role in an organization

Q14.　According to Mirvis and Hall, which of the following is an example of what one might experience in a boundaryless career, but not in a more traditional career?

    a.　a secure work environment
    b.　altruistic work
    c.　temporary assignments
    d.　unpleasant working conditions

Q15.　Difficult transitions can be most problematic for individuals if they occur in this stage of Super's model of adult career development.

    a.　crystallizing
    b.　decelerating
    c.　diffusion
    d.　maintenance

Q16.　Heppner's measure of career transitions was NOT designed to measure

    a.　confidence.
    b.　control.
    c.　interests.
    d.　readiness.

Q17.   Job loss can contribute to

    a.   decreased coping skills.
    b.   increased use of alcohol.
    c.   poor health.
    d.   all of these.

Q18.   Outplacement counselors may do any of the following EXCEPT

    a.   deal with the negative impact of job loss.
    b.   help clients assess their values.
    c.   help clients develop job search strategies.
    d.   help clients sue their former employer.

Q19.   When Kanisha is fired from her job as a physician's assistant, she thinks that her boss does not really mean it. According to Hopson and Adam's model of coping with adult transitions, she is most likely in this stage.

    a.   immobilization
    b.   minimization
    c.   search for meaning
    d.   testing out

Q20.   Jenna has just learned that after working at the ZZ Toy Company for 23 years, the plant will close in two weeks. According to Hopson and Adam's model of coping with adult transitions, she is most likely in this stage.

    a.   immobilization
    b.   minimization
    c.   letting go
    d.   self-doubt

Q21.   Caesar has been dismissed from his job. He is aware that he will not be rehired. After making some contact with potential employers, he has lined up some interviews. He is, at this point, aware not only of his own feelings about the job termination, but also how it has affected his wife and children. According to Hopson and Adam's model of coping with adult transitions, he is most likely in this stage.

    a.   maintenance
    b.   minimization
    c.   letting go
    d.   search for meaning

Q22.   Which of the following is a career situation that women, more than men, may experience?

    a.   being laid off
    b.   dealing with sexual harassment
    c.   being transferred
    d.   getting promoted

Q23. According to Shullman and Fitzgerald, which of these types of sexual harassment is considered the least severe?

    a.   being threatened with punishment if one does not engage in sexual activity
    b.   being asked to engage in a sexual activity in exchange for pay or advancement
    c.   sexist verbal remarks
    d.   sexual assault

Q24. According to Gutek and Koss, women are most likely to experience _____ immediately after being sexually harassed.

    a.   anger
    b.   confusion or self blame
    c.   depression
    d.   disillusionment

Q25. Discrimination that includes failure to promote, hire, or give pay raises is most likely to be experienced by

    a.   culturally diverse populations.
    b.   college graduates.
    c.   high school graduates.
    d.   Caucasian men.

ANSWER KEY

1.	d	11.	c	Q6.	T	Q16.	c
2.	d	12.	c	Q7.	F	Q17.	d
3.	a	13.	a	Q8.	T	Q18.	d
4.	b	14.	c	Q9.	T	Q19.	b
5.	c	15.	b	Q10.	F	Q20.	a
6.	b			Q11.	c	Q21.	d
7.	d	Q1.	F	Q12.	d	Q22.	b
8.	c	Q2.	T	Q13.	a	Q23.	c
9.	c	Q3.	F	Q14.	c	Q24.	b
10.	a	Q4.	T	Q15.	d	Q25.	a
		Q5.	T				

CHAPTER 11
CONSTRUCTIVIST AND NARRATIVE APPROACHES TO CAREER DEVELOPMENT

Constructivism

Postmodernism

Social construction

Narrative career counseling

Agent

Setting

Action

Instrument

Storytelling

Goals of assessment in narrative career counseling

Cochran's Narrative Career Counseling

1. Elaborating a career problem (vocational card sort, drawing, anecdotes)

2. Composing a life history (success experience, lifeline, career-o-gram, life chapters)

3. Eliciting a future narrative

4. Reality construction

5. Changing a life structure

6. Enacting a role

7. Crystallizing a decision

Savickas's career construction theory

Vocational personality — Holland's theory
Developmental tasks of career adaptability

Dimensions of career adaptability

Concern
Control
Curiosity
Confidence

Life themes

Lifestyle
Early recollections
Five major life tasks

Career counseling using career construction theory

Reviewing career counseling
Attending to verbs
Examining headlines of the recollections
Moving from preoccupation to occupation
Role models as suggestions for a plan
Profiling adaptability
Appraising vocational personality
Crafting a success formula
The life portrait

The role of assessment instruments

The role of occupational information

Applying the theory to women and culturally diverse populations

Counselor issues

CHAPTER 11

CONSTRUCTIVIST AND NARRATIVE APPROACHES TO CAREER DEVELOPMENT

EXERCISE 11.1

YOUR LIFE IN BOOK CHAPTERS

E. 1. Develop chapter titles for a story about your life. The chapter titles should represent accomplishments that are significant for you. Use about six to 10 chapter titles. After each, indicate the accomplishment that they represent. The chapter titles should be unique to you. For example, Teacher's Eager Assistant is more descriptive than Elementary School Years. (Narrative)

_____

_____

_____

_____

_____

_____

_____

_____

_____

_____

_____

E. 2. How well do these chapter titles represent significant areas in your life? Describe their relevance to occupations that you have considered entering. (Narrative)

_____

_____

_____

_____

EXERCISE 11.3

YOUR LIFE LINE

Using the lines below, write in significant events that have affected your career choice in the past and present. Also, write in significant events which you think may happen in the future. Because of the size limits of this book, the lifeline is divided into four segments (birth to 15 years, 16 to 30 years, 31 to 60 years, and 61 years to death).

0   **15**

16   **30**

EXERCISE 11.3 (CONTINUED)

YOUR LIFE LINE

---

31   60

---

61   ?

E. 3. How well does your lifeline summarize career choice influences and dilemmas that you have had to deal with? Explain. (Narrative)

_____

_____

_____

_____

_____

_____

E. 4. List three of your earliest recollections (from ages four to six if possible). Write the life theme or a possible direction suggested by one or more of the recollections. (Social construction theory)

_____

_____

_____

_____

_____

_____

_____

HELGA'S PARTICIPATION IN NARRATIVE CAREER COUNSELING

Helga's two children have now entered first and third grades. She has decided at the age of 31 to return to work and is in the process of arranging childcare for her children. Helga has been a cost estimator for a construction firm. Not only is she unsure that she wants to return to this type of work, but she also has second thoughts about leaving her children in the afternoons. She enjoys playing the cello and singing in a chorus. However, she sees no possibility of a career in these areas, but worries about having time to continue in these activities.

You will be using Cochran's narrative career counseling to help Helga. Please answer the following questions from that perspective.

1. From your point of view as a narrative career counselor, you would view Helga as the

    a. agent.
    b. client.
    c. editor.
    d. setting.

2. When Helga goes back and forth among staying at home with her children, considering going back to being a cost estimator, or returning to college for a Master's Degree, you see this as

    a. a career decision.
    b. an identity crisis.
    c. self-doubt.
    d. wavering

3. Which of the following would you do first as you apply Cochran's narrative career counseling approach?

    a. change a life structure
    b. elaborate a career problem
    c. elicit a future narrative
    d. reality construction

4. As you Compose a Life History, which of these are you least likely to do? Have Helga

    a. complete a lifeline.
    b. fill out a career-o-gram.
    c. write out her life in chapter titles.
    d. try out a role in a new career.

5. Which of these methods is most likely to help Helga in the Reality Construction phase of Cochran's narrative career counseling approach?

    a. drawing pictures
    b. early recollections
    c. vocational card sort
    d. volunteer work

6. When Helga enters the Changing a Life Structure phase, you would listen for a _____ to emerge.

    a. balance
    b. lifeline
    c. setting
    d. theme

7. The theme that emerges in the Changing a Life Structure phase is referred to by Cochran as a

    a. calling.
    b. career project.
    c. lifeline.
    d. vocational construct.

114

8. As you use Cochran's narrative approach in your career counseling, Helga's career related behavior outside of counseling sessions should be characterized by her

    a.   activity.
    b.   depression.
    c.   introversion.
    d.   logical career decision-making.

MARSHALL'S USE OF SAVICKAS'S SOCIAL CONSTRUCTION CAREER COUNSELING

Marshall has sought career counseling from you. You are using social construction career counseling methods with him. He has left the Army and is considering entering college. When he was in the military, he was a truck mechanic. At first, this work interested him, but later he decided that it grew boring. He has had three years of military experience since he left high school. His participation in the Army along with being stationed in South Korea and Germany has changed the way he sees himself.

Please answer these questions from the point of view of a social construction career counselor.

9. When Marshall tells you that he would enjoy designing airplane engines and figuring out which engine parts would be most efficient, you are able to learn more about his

    a.   early recollections.
    b.   disengagement issues from the military.
    c.   value system.
    d.   vocational personality

10. Marshall describes to you why he was bored fixing trucks, and why he wants to take math and engineering courses. He is beginning to specify a career direction. According to Savickas's social construction theory, he is discussing

    a.   a life theme.
    b.   some developmental tasks of career adaptability.
    c.   some dimensions of career adaptability.
    d.   moving from preoccupation to occupation.

11. The answer to question 10 is "b." Marshall is discussing some developmental tasks of career adaptability. Which task is most relevant for Marshall and characterizes his concerns?

    a.   growth
    b.   exploration
    c.   establishment
    d.   management

12. Marshall came to see you because he is unsure about his ability to make career choices. Although he is thinking that engineering may be a good career choice for him, he is anxious that he will not be successful in doing it. Which dimension of career adaptability is he discussing?

    a.   concern
    b.   control
    c.   curiosity
    d.   confidence

13. When Marshall tells you of a time when he was six years old and he solved a puzzle that his eight-year-old brother couldn't solve, he tells you of the satisfaction that he felt. Marshall told you this when you asked him to tell you

    a.   his lifestyle.
    b.   an early recollection.
    c.   about his hobbies.
    d.   about a preoccupation.

14. As Marshall tells you the story of his life and his goals for his future, you attend to his use of

    a.   adjectives, because they show emotion.
    b.   nouns, because they are specific.
    c.   compound sentences, because they show complexity of thought.
    d.   verbs, because they are action words.

15. To make a bridge from a variety of views that Marshall has and to bring together many stories he has told you, you will write out and share with Marshall

    a.   your formula for his vocational personality.
    b.   your view of his life portrait.
    c.   your view of his most important early recollections.
    d.   the five major life tasks he must complete.

APPLYING NARRATIVE AND SOCIAL CAREER CONSTRUCTION APPROACHES TO MEN AND WOMEN

Does Cochran's narrative approach to career counseling have different implications for men and women? Explain.

_____

_____

_____

_____

_____

What implications does Cochran's narrative approach to career counseling have for counseling people from diverse populations?

_____

_____

_____

Does the social career construction approach to career counseling have different implications for men and women? Explain.

_____

_____

_____

_____

What implications does the social career construction approach to career counseling have for counseling people from diverse populations?

_____

_____

_____

STRENGTHS AND LIMITATIONS

What do you see as the strengths and limitations of Cochran's narrative approach to career counseling?

Strengths	Limitations
_____	_____
_____	_____
_____	_____
_____	_____

What do you see as the strengths and limitations of the social career construction approach to career counseling?

Strengths   Limitations

_____   _____

_____   _____

_____   _____

_____   _____

_____   _____

NARRATIVE AND SOCIAL CAREER CONSTRUCTION APPROACHES TO CAREER DEVELOPMENT: A QUIZ

True or false items: Decide if the following items are more "true" or more "false" as they apply to concepts discussed in this chapter.

T   F   Q1.   Postmodernism is the view that individuals construct their own view of events.

T   F   Q2.   Social constructionism includes the study of how interactions with others affect people's view of the world.

T   F   Q3.   The "setting" is a concept associated with narrative career counseling.

T   F   Q4.   Planning for the future is an appropriate goal for narrative career counseling.

T   F   Q5.   For narrative career counseling to be successful there should be a discrepancy between what the current situation is and what the client wants it to be.

T   F   Q6.   The lifeline is an appropriate exercise to use in Cochran's narrative career counseling.

T   F   Q7.   Like Super's theory of career counseling, crystallizing a career choice appears at the beginning of Cochran's narrative career counseling,

T   F   Q8.   In his career construction theory, Savickas does NOT make use of other career theories.

T   F   Q9.   Savickas's developmental tasks of career adaptability include Super's growth, exploration, and establishment stages.

T   F   Q10. In Savickas's career construction theory of career counseling, the counselor presents a verbal or written life portrait to the client.

Multiple choice items: Select the best answer from the alternatives given. Answer each question from the point of view of theories of adult career crises and transitions.

Q11.   According to constructivist philosophy, rationalists are individuals who believe

    a.   in the value of scientific proof.
    b.   interests, abilities, and values are important in career decision-making.
    c.   that individual values should not change over time.
    d.   that there is no fixed truth.

Q12.   Postmodernism is a philosophy that values the importance of

    a.   attending to new changes in the world of work.
    b.   making career decisions that follow careful decision-making procedures.
    c.   recognizing that individuals can have their own view of what is real for them.
    d.   scientific proof in evaluating ideas and events.

Q13.   According to narrative career counseling, one's career has which two important elements?

    a.   ability and interests
    b.   action and time
    c.   constructs and unity
    d.   majors and occupations

Q14.   According to narrative career counseling, which of these would not be an instrument?

    a.   coworkers
    b.   friends
    c.   a spouse
    d.   the client

Q15.   In narrative career counseling, wavering presents an opportunity for the client to

    a.   determine the future direction of the story.
    b.   change the agent of the story.
    c.   develop a fictional story.
    d.   decide not to continue with career counseling.

Q16.   In narrative career assessment, the counselor's role is most like that of a(an)

    a.   author.
    b.   editor.
    c.   lighting designer.
    d.   producer.

Q17. Which of the following is not a technique associated with describing a life history in narrative career counseling?

    a.   career-o-gram
    b.   life chapters
    c.   success experiences
    d.   early recollections

Q18. In narrative career counseling, which one of these activities would fit best with learning about being a lawyer?

    a.   fantasizing about being a lawyer
    b.   reading about being a lawyer
    c.   visiting lawyers at work
    d.   watching a drama about lawyers

Q19. In narrative career counseling, cultural narratives can represent

    a.   cultural stereotypes.
    b.   career projects.
    c.   cultural careers.
    d.   the agent.

Q20. Savickas uses _____ theory as a way of viewing vocational personality in his social constructionist career theory.

    a.   Gottfredson's
    b.   Holland's
    c.   Myer's-Briggs
    d.   work adjustment

Q21. Which of the following are examples of developmental tasks used in Savickas's social constructionist career theory?

    a.   exploration and curiosity
    b.   exploration and establishment
    c.   introversion and extraversion
    d.   introversion and moratorium

Q22. In Savickas's social constructionist career theory, which one of these is NOT a dimension of career adaptability?

    a.   concern
    b.   control
    c.   confidence
    d.   crystallization

Q23. In listening to the client's story, Savickas listens for

a. congruent elements in the story.
b. role of actions of others.
c. a life theme.
d. the client's search for meaning.

Q24. Savickas listens for five major life tasks. Which list includes the five major life tasks?

a. self-development, spiritual development, occupation, society, and love
b. support, information, systematic decision-making, knowledge, and performance
c. change, letting go, testing out, search for meaning, and internalization
d. growth, exploration, establishment, maintenance (management), and disengagement

Q25. In a career style interview, Savickas would ask clients to describe all but which one of the following?

a. favorite book.
b. hobbies.
c. a role model.
d. scores on the Scholastic Aptitude Test.

ANSWER KEY

1.	a	11.	b	Q6.	T	Q16.	b
2.	d	12.	d	Q7.	F	Q17.	d
3.	b	13.	b	Q8.	F	Q18.	c
4.	d	14.	d	Q9.	T	Q19.	a
5.	d	15.	b	Q10.	T	Q20.	b
6.	d			Q11.	a	Q21.	b
7.	b	Q1.	T	Q12.	c	Q22.	d
8.	a	Q2.	T	Q13.	b	Q23.	c
9.	d	Q3.	T	Q14.	d	Q24.	a
10.	b	Q4.	T	Q15.	a	Q25.	d
		Q5.	T				

CHAPTER 12
RELATIONAL APPROACHES TO CAREER DEVELOPMENT

Roe's personality theory

The three types of parental attitudes

Concentration on the child

Avoidance of the child

Acceptance of the child

Relationship of parental style to occupational selection

Research support

Attachment theory

Three types of responding

Secure pattern
Anxious-ambivalent pattern
Avoidant pattern

Parent–child career interactions

Joint action

Parent Involved Career Exploration (PICE)

1. Introduction

2. Pattern identification exercises (PIE)

3. Discussion of school preferences and performance

4. A perspective on education and labor market possibilities

5. Planning the next step

Family systems therapy

Enmeshed family

Disengaged family

Genograms

Phillips's developmental relationship model

Actions of others

Nonactive support

Unconditional support

Information provided

Alternatives provided

Push-nudge

Forced guidance

Criticism

Self-directedness

Confident independence (false confidence)

Unsuccessful recruitment

Insecure use of others

Cautious

Seeking information

Weighing opinion

Sounding board

Systematic

Applying the theories to women and culturally diverse populations

CHAPTER 12

RELATIONAL APPROACHES TO CAREER DEVELOPMENT

EXERCISE 12.1

RELATIONSHIPS AND CAREER CHOICE

E. 1. In what ways have your mother (or other female parental figure) influenced or affected your career choice? (Roe, Parent-Child Care Interaction)

_____

_____

_____

_____

_____

E. 2. In what ways have your father (or other male parental figure) influenced or affected your career choice? (Roe, Parent-Child Care Interaction)

_____

_____

_____

_____

_____

E. 3. How has the quality of your relationship with your parents affected your career choice?

_____

_____

_____

_____

_____

_____

E. 4. List three ways the actions of others (through criticism, telling you what to do, providing choices or information, or support) have influenced your career choice. What is your relationship to that person (for example, friend, parent, teacher, and so forth)? (Phillips's Developmental Relational Model-Action of Others)

_____

_____

_____

_____

E. 5. List three examples of relying (or not relying) on others in your career decision-making. For example, do you use others as a sounding board, do you get information from them about you, are you afraid to not use others, or do you not use their opinion at all? (Phillips's Developmental Relational Model-Self-Directedness)

_____

_____

_____

_____

COUNSELING ALI USING PHILLIPS'S DEVELOPMENTAL RELATIONAL APPROACH TO CAREER COUNSELING

Ali graduated high school two years ago. He took college preparatory courses just in case he would apply to college some day, but he decided not to go and went to work in the mall in a large sporting goods store. He thought it would be fun as he liked sports and had been on soccer and basketball teams in high school. What he had thought would be fun is now boring. He likes the people that he works with and enjoys what some of his managers do. However, he sees people with a college education moving into management positions. He is the oldest in his family. He has two younger sisters in high school. His mother is a customer service representative for a large bank. His father is in jail for five more years because he committed armed robbery. His mother values the additional income that Ali brings in to support the family.

1. As Ali talks to you about whether to return to college, look for another job in retailing, or stay at his current job, you become aware that he has many people in his life that he listens to, although with varying amounts of attention. You then start to think of assessing these influences. You are attending to which of Phillips's major themes?

    a.   Actions of Others
    b.   Self-Directedness

124

2. Ali's mother is annoyed that Ali would even consider leaving his job. She tells him that things are going well now and that his salary is helping her a lot in raising the girls. When he brings up college, she finds fault with his arguments about going to college. According to Phillips's developmental relational model, Ali's mother's Actions of Others would be called

    a.   criticism.
    b.   push-nudge.
    c.   information provided.
    d.   unconditional support.

3. When Ali discusses his career choice with his girlfriend, Ramona, she says, "Do what you want. Only you know what is best for you. I don't have a clue." According to Phillips's developmental relational model, Ramona's Actions of Others would be called

    a.   criticism.
    b.   information provided.
    c.   non-active support.
    d.   push-nudge.

4. Ali has become friendly with the manager of the store that he works in. The manager has given him some descriptions about how he and others have become store managers. According to Phillips's developmental relational model, the store manager's Actions of Others would be called

    a.   criticism.
    b.   information provided.
    c.   non-active support.
    d.   push-nudge.

5. When Ali talks to his high school math teacher about what he might do with his career plan, his teacher mentions some possibilities in engineering and math, alternatives that he had not thought of, but would be occupations he could enter if he goes to college. According to Phillips's developmental relational model, Ali's math teacher's Actions of Others would be called

    a.   alternatives provided.
    b.   criticism.
    c.   forced guidance.
    d.   push-nudge.

6. Once a month Ali visits his father in prison. He has had a good relationship with his father, when his father is sober. His father's unpredictable behavior scares him. However, he has noticed that his father is more philosophical now that he is in prison. His father is proud of Ali and appreciative of his support of his wife and daughters. Yet he also realizes that Ali needs to do what is best for Ali. He is pleased to hear that Ali is considering college. He talks to him about how he could help Ali financially when he gets out of prison. According to Phillips's developmental relational model, Ali's father's Actions of Others would be called

    a.   alternatives provided.
    b.   push-nudge.
    c.   non-active support.
    d.   unconditional support.

7. When you talk to Ali, you are pleased that he is seeking information. You encourage his career decision-making and his interest in returning to college. You are also aware of his family's financial problems and the need to consider how he will handle them. According to Phillips's developmental relational model, your Actions of Others would be called

    a. alternatives provided.
    b. forced guidance.
    c. non-active support.
    d. unconditional support.

When talking to Ali, he discusses past career decisions that he has made. He also describes how he has involved his parents and others in his career decision-making. As you listen to him, you think of Phillips's categories of Self-Directedness. This helps you to follow his decision-making process.

8. When Ali was in ninth grade, he had decided that he wanted to be a professional basketball player. His teammates didn't say anything to him about this, although they doubted he could do it. According to Phillips's developmental relational model, Ali's category of Self-Directedness can be called

    a. cautious.
    b. confident independence (false confidence).
    c. insecure use of others.
    d. systematic.

9. In tenth grade, Ali felt a little silly about having told others that he wanted to be a professional basketball player. He then changed his career decision-making style abruptly and became very reluctant to either think or talk about career possibilities. According to Phillips's developmental relational model, Ali's category of Self-Directedness can be classified as

    a. cautious.
    b. insecure use of others.
    c. sounding board.
    d. weighing options.

10. When Ali was in high school, he felt that his parents had been of no use in helping him figure out what he should do. He was upset that his father had legal troubles and his mother seemed so worried about his sisters. He didn't know who to turn to for advice. According to Phillips's developmental relational model, Ali's category of Self-Directedness can be classified as

    a. cautious.
    b. insecure use of others.
    c. sounding board.
    d. unsuccessful recruitment.

11. During the last year, Ali has asked his math teacher and his best friend about what he seems to do well. Both his friend and his teacher were supportive of his math abilities. Additionally, his friend talked about his ability to listen to others and make them feel comfortable. According to Phillips's developmental relational model, Ali's category of Self-Directedness can be classified as

    a.   insecure use of others.
    b.   seeking information about self.
    c.   systematic.
    d.   unsuccessful recruitment.

12. Ali has sought your advice about what to do, as he values your advice. He wants to consider the different things that he might do next year. He is not clear exactly what to do, but he knows he needs to consider different possibilities. According to Phillips's developmental relational model, Ali's category of Self-Directedness can be classified as

    a.   cautious.
    b.   insecure use of others.
    c.   weighing options.
    d.   systematic.

13. Talking to his best friend about what he might do next year has helped him think through his career decision more clearly. According to Phillips's developmental relational model, Ali's category of Self-Directedness can be classified as

    a.   cautious.
    b.   weighing options.
    c.   sounding board.
    d.   systematic.

14. As Ali talks to you more about his career decision-making, he is very thoughtful. He listens carefully to what you have to say, but takes responsibility for his decision-making. He discusses his interests, abilities, and values with you. According to Phillips's developmental relational model, Ali's category of Self-Directedness can be classified as

    a.   cautious.
    b.   sounding board.
    c.   systematic.
    d.   weighing options.

APPLYING ATTACHMENT THEORY AND PHILLIPS'S DEVELOPMENTAL RELATIONAL MODEL TO MEN, WOMEN, AND CULTURALLY DIVERSE GROUPS

Does attachment theory have different implications for the career development of men and women? Explain.

_____

_____

_____

_____

_____

Does Phillips's developmental relational model have different implications for males and females? Explain.

_____

_____

_____

_____

_____

What implications does attachment theory have for career counseling with individuals from diverse populations?

_____

_____

_____

_____

_____

What implications does Phillips's developmental relational model have for counseling individuals from diverse populations?

_____

_____

_____

_____

STRENGTHS AND LIMITATIONS

What do you see as the strengths and limitations of attachment theory's application to career counseling?

Strengths	Limitations
_____	_____
_____	_____
_____	_____
_____	_____
_____	_____

What do you see as the strengths and limitations of Phillips's developmental relational model theory?

Strengths	Limitations
_____	_____
_____	_____
_____	_____
_____	_____

RELATIONAL APPROACHES TO CAREER DEVELOPMENT: A QUIZ

True or false items: Decide if the following items are more "true" or more "false" as they apply to concepts discussed in this chapter.

T F Q1. Relational career development theorists believe that the most important factor in choosing a career is the parent's influence on their child's career choice.

T　F　Q2.　Roe hypothesized that you could predict later occupational entry of children by knowing the child raising attitudes of their parents.

T　F　Q3.　Research supports Roe's theory of occupational selection.

T　F　Q4.　An application of attachment theory to career development is that concerns about attachment to parents in childhood can cause anxiety in career exploration.

T　F　Q5.　The Parent Involved Career Exploration Counseling Process differs from most career counseling procedures in that parents are included in the career counseling process.

T　F　Q6.　The genogram is a technique from family therapy that can be used in career counseling.

T　F　Q7.　Phillips's developmental relational model differs from other relationship models of career development in that it is not limited to research on child-parent issues.

T　F　Q8.　All relational models, including Phillips's, take the view that the parents should determine the occupation of the child, because of the parent's world of work experience.

T　F　Q9.　In Phillips's developmental relational model, Actions of Others range from confident independence (false confidence) to systematic.

T　F　Q10.　Relational models do not incorporate trait and factor theory in their work, but present a model in direct opposition to it.

Multiple choice items: Select the best answer from the alternatives given. Answer each question from the point of view of relational models of career development.

Q11.　Roe's classification system of parental attitudes towards children includes all but which one of the following?

　　　a.　acceptance of the child
　　　b.　avoidance of the child
　　　c.　concentration on the child
　　　d.　discipline of the child

Q12.　Anne Roe wanted to prove that

　　　a.　attachment style affects career choice.
　　　b.　genograms were useful in predicting career entry.
　　　c.　people in occupations have a common background in the way they were raised.
　　　d.　the interaction between adolescent children and their parents predicts career choice.

Q13.　Which of the following is NOT a (an) attachment pattern that is observed in children?

　　　a.　anxious
　　　b.　avoidant
　　　c.　resentful
　　　d.　secure

Q14.   From the point of view of attachment theory, career counselors offer a (an)

        a.   rationale for the selection of occupations.
        b.   opportunity to discuss parental child raising attitudes.
        c.   opportunity to discuss work adjustment issues.
        d.   secure atmosphere to discuss their career concerns.

Q15.   The study of the discussion of career concerns between parent and child is an example of a type
        of research called

        a.   assessment.
        b.   attachment.
        c.   enmeshment.
        d.   joint action.

Q16.   Researchers who study parent-career child interactions in career development are interested most
        in

        a.   assessment of abilities, interests, and values.
        b.   how conversations between parents and their children affect children's career views.
        c.   identifying secure attachment patterns of children.
        d.   the enmeshment that occurs within the families interactions...

Q17.   The Pattern Identification Exercise includes a discussion of a (an)

        a.   attachment issue.
        b.   leisure activity.
        c.   occupation.
        d.   problem between parent and child.

Q18.   Family therapists have used the concepts of disengagement and _____ to examine career
        development of children and adolescents.

        a.   assessment
        b.   engagement
        c.   enmeshment
        d.   resentment

Q19.   Cheryl has decided that she will be a politician. She has this idea from watching political
        campaigns on television. She has not talked to anyone else about this idea and does not plan to.
        According to Phillips's developmental relational model, Cheryl's category of Self-Directedness
        can be labeled as

        a.   cautious.
        b.   confident independence (false confidence).
        c.   seeking information about self.
        d.   systematic.

131

Q20.   Her high school biology teacher has told Meifen that she will not let Meifen take the advanced biology class because of her C- in her first biology course. According to Phillips's developmental relational model, Meifen's category of Actions of Others can be labeled as

   a.   criticism.
   b.   forced guidance.
   c.   non-active support.
   d.   unconditional support.

Q21.   A person who lets someone watch what she does at work (job shadowing) is likely to fulfill this role of Actions of Others according to Phillips's developmental relational model.

   a.   alternatives provided
   b.   information provided
   c.   sounding board
   d.   weighing options

Q22.   The concept of anxious-ambivalent pattern is associated with this relational theory.

   a.   attachment
   b.   family therapy
   c.   Phillips's developmental relational model
   d.   Roe's personality development theory

Q23.   The concept of concentration on the child is associated with this relational theory.

   a.   attachment
   b.   family therapy
   c.   Phillips's developmental relational model
   d.   Roe's personality development theory

Q24.   The concept of enmeshment pattern is associated with this relational theory.

   a.   family therapy
   b.   parent-child career interaction approach
   c.   Phillips's developmental relational model
   d.   Roe's personality development theory

Q25.   Which of the following is NOT an example of a relational approach to career development?

   a.   attachment theory
   b.   Myers-Briggs type theory
   c.   Phillips's developmental relational model
   d.   Roe's personality development theory

ANSWER KEY

1.	a	11.	b	Q6.	T	Q16.	b
2.	a	12.	c	Q7.	T	Q17.	b
3.	c	13.	c	Q8.	F	Q18.	c
4.	b	14.	c	Q9.	F	Q19.	b
5.	a			Q10.	F	Q20.	b
6.	d	Q1.	F	Q11.	d	Q21.	b
7.	d	Q2.	T	Q12.	c	Q22.	a
8.	b	Q3.	F	Q13.	c	Q23.	d
9.	a	Q4.	T	Q14.	d	Q24.	a
10.	d	Q5.	T	Q15.	d	Q25.	b

133

CHAPTER 13
KRUMBOLTZ'S SOCIAL LEARNING THEORY

Bandura's social learning theory

Triadic reciprocal interaction system

Genetic endowment

Environmental conditions and events
    Social factors
    Educational conditions
    Occupational conditions

Learning experiences
    Instrumental
    Observational

Task approach skills

Client cognitive and behavioral skills
    Self-observation generalizations about abilities
    Self-observation generalizations about interests
    Self-observation generalizations about values
    Generalizations about the world
    Task approach skills used in career decision-making

Counselor behavioral strategies
    Reinforcement
    Role models
    Role-playing
    Simulation

Cognitive strategies for counseling
    Goal clarification
    Counter a troublesome belief
    Look for inconsistencies between words and actions
    Cognitive rehearsal

Social learning theory goals for career counseling

Three criteria that influence goals of career counseling

Need to expand capabilities and interests
Need to prepare for changing work talks
Need to be empowered to take action

Planned happenstance theory
    Skills helpful in dealing with chance career opportunities

    Curiosity
    Persistence
    Flexibility
    Optimism
    Risk taking

Four steps in planned happenstance theory
1. Normalize planned happenstance in the client's history
2. Assist clients to transform curiosity into opportunities for learning and exploration
3. Teach clients to produce desirable chance events
4. Teach clients to overcome blocks to action

Career Beliefs Inventory can assess beliefs that are potential problems

The role of occupational information
    Job experience kits
    Computer simulation of occupations

The role of assessment instruments
    Values and interest inventories and ability tests can be used
    Career Beliefs Inventory has 25 scales

Applying social learning theory to women

Applying social learning theory to culturally diverse populations

Counselor issues

CHAPTER 13

KRUMBOLTZ'S SOCIAL LEARNING THEORY

EXERCISE 13.1

CAREER BELIEFS AND LEARNING EXPERIENCES

E. 1. What types of learning experiences (both inside and outside of school) have affected your career choices? Examples may include watching others, doing certain types of tasks, and observations about yourself. (Learning Experiences)

_____

_____

_____

_____

_____

E. 2. How has doing things well affected your interest in an activity or your desire to continue doing the activity? (Reinforcement)

_____

_____

_____

_____

_____

E. 3. How has doing things poorly affected your interest in an activity or your desire to continue doing the activity? (Reinforcement)

_____

_____

_____

_____

_____

E. 4. Give an example of a belief that you had that kept you from pursuing an activity. (Example: "I am not smart enough to be an electrical engineer"). (Counter a Troublesome Belief)

_____

_____

_____

_____

E. 5. Describe an occasion when you took advantage of a chance event that furthered your career choice. (Example: "When I was babysitting for a divorced mother, her ten-year-old daughter talked to me about missing her father. She seemed to like our talk and then I thought I could be a counselor or social worker"). (Planned Happenstance)

_____

_____

_____

_____

_____

COUNSELING GLORIA USING KRUMBOLTZ'S COGNITIVE AND BEHAVIORAL CONCEPTS AND TECHNIQUES

Gloria is a sophomore in high school who lives in Orlando, Florida. Her mother works as a food service manager at Disney World and her father is a heating and air conditioning specialist. She has a younger sister in seventh grade. Gloria's mother is concerned that Gloria is not doing well in school. When Gloria finishes school in the afternoon, she usually visits with friends. This year she is playing soccer. Gloria's father wonders if Gloria will want to go to a college. He worries about the financial pressure that he will have to help pay for college.

At her parent's request, Gloria makes an appointment to talk to you about her future plans. You will be trying to help her by using Krumboltz's social learning theory.

1. Gloria is somewhat annoyed because her parents requested that she see you. First, she talks about not needing to plan what she will do. Later as you talk more about attending college, you ask if she would like you to help her figure out whether or not to go to college and to tentatively plan what she might do if she goes to college. She likes that idea and starts to work with you to figure out what to do. According to Krumboltz, the strategy that you are using with Gloria is

   a. cognitive rehearsal.
   b. countering a troublesome belief.
   c. goal clarification.
   d. looking for inconsistencies between words and actions.

2. Gloria tells you that she likes writing papers for English class. She feels left out because she doesn't know of anyone else who likes to do that. She also writes poetry in her spare time. According to Krumboltz, she is having this kind of learning experience.

   a. associative
   b. instrumental
   c. objective
   d. occupational

3. Gloria enjoys listening to her English teacher describe plays that she has seen in New York City. In this way Gloria is learning about drama. According to Krumboltz, she is having this kind of learning experience.

   a. associative
   b. instrumental
   c. objective
   d. occupational

4. Gloria discusses her interest in going to plays and in reading literature. According to Krumboltz, she is having this kind of learning experience.

   a. self-observation generalization about abilities
   b. self-observation generalizations about interest
   c. generalizations about the world
   d. task approach skills used in career decision-making

5. Gloria is pleased to feel good about her accomplishments in English class. She gets A's on her papers as well as compliments from her teacher. According to Krumboltz, she is having this kind of learning experience.

   a. self-observation generalization about abilities
   b. self-observation generalization about interests
   c. generalizations about the world
   d. task approach skills used in career decision-making

6. Gloria talks about her uncle who is a reporter on a local newspaper. She says "I could never do that. It is too difficult for me to write under pressure." You reply "Gloria, if you had practice writing articles, you might find that you can work with time deadlines." According to Krumboltz, you are

   a. countering a troublesome belief.
   b. looking for inconsistencies between words and actions.
   c. doing cognitive rehearsal.
   d. reinforcing Gloria.

7. Gloria says to you that she really needs to find out more about time deadlines and what reporters do to deal with pressure. When you see her the following week, she says she never got around to talking to her uncle or anyone else about what they do. You point out what she had hoped to learn from talking to her uncle. She understands that she wants to do this and does so the following week. According to Krumboltz, you are

   a. countering a troublesome belief.
   b. looking for inconsistencies between words and actions.
   c. doing cognitive rehearsal.
   d. reinforcing Gloria.

8. When Gloria comes to talk to you the following week, you are pleased to hear her talk about how she visited her uncle at work and learned how he and other reporters work. You say "That's great Gloria, you really learned a lot by taking that trip to the paper." According to Krumboltz, you are

   a. countering a troublesome belief.
   b. looking for inconsistencies between words and actions.
   c. reinforcing Gloria.
   d. role-playing.

9. Gloria has several interests. She says that she has always enjoyed working with her father on projects around the home. She has enjoyed helping him build cabinets and fix plumbing. She says "I could never tell him this. He thinks a girl would be crazy to do that kind of stuff for a living." You talk with her about discussing this with her father. To prepare for a talk with her father, Gloria pretends to be her father while you play her. According to Krumboltz, you are

   a. countering a troublesome belief.
   b. doing role-playing.
   c. doing simulation.
   d. doing cognitive rehearsal.

10. Gloria talks about going to shop class and having an opportunity to try out some complex wood working equipment. According to Krumboltz, Gloria is doing this.

   a. countering a troublesome belief
   b. doing role-playing
   c. doing simulation
   d. doing cognitive rehearsal

138

11. Gloria talks to you about the possibility of going to a vocational school next year to study carpentry. She is enthusiastic but seems impulsive. You are concerned about her

    a.   self-observation generalizations about her abilities.
    b.   self-observation generalizations about her interests.
    c.   self-observation generalizations about her values.
    d.   task-approach skills.

12. The following week Gloria comes into your office and says "You will never believe what happened. I was at this football game and I was talking to this senior guy I know who says that he is a stringer for a local newspaper and writes up the high points of this game. So he shows me what he does and he says can I cover a game for him this week. He told me to bring him what I write and he will see I get paid. I think it's neat." You are pleased to hear this and then you ask how she has dealt with other chance events in her past. According to Krumboltz, you are

    a.   normalizing planned happenstance in the client's history.
    b.   assisting the client to transform curiosity into opportunities for learning and exploration.
    c.   teaching the client to produce observational activities.
    d.   teaching the client to overcome blocks to action.

13. When Gloria tells you that she has learned a lot not only from this experience, but also from times she has helped out an uncle in his gas station, you talk about what she learned from these examples. Gloria talks about how much she learned from writing up a football game, even though she doesn't care much about football. You help her understand what she has learned about writing an article for a newspaper. According to Krumboltz, you are

    a.   normalizing planned happenstance in the client's history.
    b.   assisting the client to transform curiosity into opportunities for learning and exploration.
    c.   teaching the client to produce desirable chance events.
    d.   teaching the client to overcome blocks to action.

14. When you and Gloria talk about writing a brief sports report, you also talk about other ways she can learn about writing, such as the school newspaper and where that could lead. By making these suggestions to Gloria, you are, according to Krumboltz,

    a.   normalizing planned happenstance in the client's history.
    b.   assisting the client to transform curiosity into opportunities for learning and exploration.
    c.   teaching the client to produce desirable chance events.
    d.   teaching the client to overcome blocks to action.

15. Gloria also talks about wanting to explore more possibilities in occupations like cabinet making. You support her ideas to help her father be less resistant to her exploration of this field and more open to involving her in his hobbies. You want her to continue to be curious, persistent, flexible, optimistic, and risk taking. According to Krumboltz, you are

    a.   normalizing planned happenstance in the client's history.
    b.   assisting the client to transform curiosity into opportunities for learning and exploration.
    c.   teaching the client to produce desirable chance events.
    d.   teaching the client to overcome blocks to action.

APPLYING KRUMBOLTZ'S SOCIAL LEARNING THEORY TO MEN, WOMEN, AND CULTURALLY DIVERSE GROUPS

Does Krumboltz's social learning theory have different implications for the career development of men and women? Explain.

_____

_____

_____

_____

_____

_____

What implications does Krumboltz's social learning theory have for career counseling with individuals from diverse populations?

_____

_____

_____

_____

_____

_____

STRENGTHS AND LIMITATIONS

What do you see as the strengths and limitations of the application of Krumboltz's social learning theory to career counseling?

Strengths	Limitations
_____	_____
_____	_____
_____	_____
_____	_____
_____	_____

140

140

KRUMBOLTZ'S SOCIAL LEARNING THEORY: A QUIZ

True or false items: Decide if the following items are more "true" or more "false" as they apply to concepts discussed in this chapter.

T   F   Q1.   Bandura believed that biological influences were more important to personality development than learning experiences.

T   F   Q2.   Playing trombone in an orchestra is an example of an instrumental learning experience rather than an associative one.

T   F   Q3.   A critic's review of a comedian's performance would be an example of self-observation generalizations about abilities.

T   F   Q4.   Krumboltz's social learning theory as it relates to career development only focuses on self-observations, not observations about the world.

T   F   Q5.   By watching a role model, such as a professional basketball player, a young person can have an instrumental learning experience.

T   F   Q6.   Role-playing a job information interview is one means for clients to learn new behaviors.

T   F   Q7.   When counselors point out inaccuracies in clients' beliefs, this is consistent with Krumboltz's social learning view of career counseling.

T   F   Q8.   For counselors to teach clients to mentally rehearse positive statements before saying them is consistent with Krumboltz's social learning view of career counseling.

T   F   Q9.   Taking advantage of a chance meeting with an employer is an example of planned happenstance.

T   F   Q10. Clients don't need to be taught how to take advantage of planned happenstance, it occurs automatically.

Multiple choice items: Select the best answer from the alternatives given. Answer each question from the point of view Krumboltz's social learning theory.

Q11.   According to Bandura, the triadic reciprocal interaction system refers to interaction among all of the following EXCEPT

    a.   behavior
    b.   environment
    c.   personal factors
    d.   philosophy

Q12. Environmental factors are important in Krumboltz's theory. Which of these is NOT an example of an environmental factor?

    a.   associative learning experiences
    b.   educational conditions
    c.   occupational conditions
    d.   social factors

Q13. According to Krumboltz, instrumental learning experiences are made up of

    a.   abilities, interests, and values.
    b.   antecedents, behavior, and consequences.
    c.   behavior, environmental factors, and personal factors.
    d.   secure, anxious, and avoidant patterns.

Q14. According to Krumboltz, which of the following is an example of a task approach skill?

    a.   graduation from high school
    b.   curiosity
    c.   energy
    d.   values clarification

Q15. According to Krumboltz, which of these would be an example of generalizations about the world?

    a.   generalizations about operating a bakery
    b.   generalizations about liking being a baker
    c.   generalizations about having the ability to be a baker
    d.   generalizations about valuing being a baker

Q16. When the client practices how to have a graduate school admissions interview with a counselor, this is called

    a.   goal setting.
    b.   reinforcement.
    c.   role-playing.
    d.   simulation.

Q17. Which of these is the most commonly used behavioral career counseling technique?

    a.   goal setting.
    b.   reinforcement.
    c.   role-playing.
    d.   simulation.

Q18. When a client says that there are no jobs in the field of magazine publication, this is an example of

    a.   cognitive rehearsal.
    b.   an inconsistency between words and actions.
    c.   a troublesome belief.
    d.   reinforcement.

Q19. According to Krumboltz's theory, the major goal of career counseling is to

    a.   assess one's interests and abilities.
    b.   avoid planned happenstance.
    c.   choose a career.
    d.   learn about one's self and one's environment.

Q20. In his discussion of criteria that influence goals of career counseling , Krumboltz believes people should

    a.   assume the stability of occupations.
    b.   be given a diagnosis as to their career problems.
    c.   expand their capabilities and interests.
    d.   make career decisions based on interests alone.

Q21. Planned happenstance encourages

    a.   caution in career decision-making.
    b.   developing a calling.
    c.   open-mindedness.
    d.   reliance on the opinions of others.

Q22. In dealing with planned happenstance, Krumboltz believes that all but one of these is an important asset.

    a.   curiosity
    b.   flexibility
    c.   risk taking
    d.   security

Q23. According to Krumboltz, which of these is most helpful in assisting clients in dealing with unplanned events?

    a.   attend to attachment issues with parents
    b.   avoid risks which might produce chance events
    c.   follow a sequence of events to produce a planned outcome
    d.   learn to produce desirable chance events

Q24. Krumboltz's Career Beliefs Inventory contains scales that measure

a. 25 perceptions that could be problems for clients.
b. interests in 25 occupations.
c. scores on 25 types of planned happenstance.
d. views on 25 common work values.

Q25. In examining the appropriateness of a counselor to work with a specific client, Krumboltz is concerned that the client's problems fit within the counselor's area of

a. expertise.
b. instrumental learning.
c. planned happenstance.
d. triadic reciprocal interaction system.

ANSWER KEY

1.	c	11.	d	Q6.	T	Q16.	c
2.	b	12.	a	Q7.	T	Q17.	b
3.	a	13.	b	Q8.	T	Q18.	c
4.	b	14.	c	Q9.	T	Q19.	d
5.	a	15.	d	Q10.	F	Q20.	c
6.	a	Q1.	F	Q11.	d	Q21.	c
7.	b	Q2.	T	Q12.	a	Q22.	d
8.	c	Q3.	F	Q13.	b	Q23.	d
9.	b	Q4.	F	Q14.	d	Q24.	a
10.	c	Q5.	F	Q15.	a	Q25.	a

144

CHAPTER 14
SOCIAL COGNITIVE CAREER THEORY

Based on Bandura's social learning theory

Uses triadic reciprocal interaction system

Self-efficacy

                                Social cognitive model of the development of interests

Outcome expectations

Goals

                                Social cognitive model of performance

Contextual factors

                                Social cognitive model of work and satisfaction

    Barriers

    Supports

                                The role of occupational information

The social cognitive career model of career choice

    Self-efficacy → Interest

                                  The role of assessment instruments

    Outcome expectations → Interest

    Interest → Choice goals

                                  Applying social cognitive career theory to women

    Goals → Choice actions

    Choice actions → Performance outcomes

                                  Applying social cognitive career theory to culturally diverse populations

    Performance outcomes → Learning experiences → Self-efficacy/Outcome expectations

    Outcome expectations → Choice goals → Choice Actions

                                  Counselor issues

                →Interest

    Self-efficacy → Choice actions

                → Performance outcomes

CHAPTER 14

SOCIAL COGNITIVE CAREER THEORY

EXERCISE 14.1

SELF-EFFICACY, OUTCOMES, AND GOALS

E. 1. How has your judgment about your ability to do well academically changed over the past five years? (Self-Efficacy)

_____

_____

_____

_____

E. 2. How has your judgment about your ability to achieve your current career choice changed over the past few years? (Self-Efficacy)

_____

_____

_____

_____

E. 3. What type of work do you believe that you will be doing in the next few years? Describe some of the tasks. (Outcome Expectations)

_____

_____

_____

_____

_____

146

E. 4. What do you want to be doing in ten years? (Goals)

_____

_____

_____

E. 5. What factors have helped you move towards your current career choice? (Support)

_____

_____

_____

_____

E. 6. What factors have interfered with obtaining your current career choice? (Barriers)

_____

_____

_____

_____

_____

COUNSELING KELVIN USING SOCIAL COGNITIVE CAREER THEORY

Kelvin is an African American high school junior from Biloxi, Mississippi. His parents moved there six years ago from central Mississippi where his father was a sharecropper and grew vegetables and tobacco. Kelvin and his four brothers and sisters are now attending school in a larger school system than they did in rural Mississippi. Kelvin had never thought about what he might do when he became an adult, other than farming. He had helped his father with farm equipment when he was younger. Now he helps neighbors fix their cars. He has found school to be more challenging since he entered high school. Presently, at 16, he is wondering about dropping out of school. Currently, he is working in a supermarket where he is employed for 15 hours per week.

One of Kelvin's teachers asks that you, his guidance counselor, talk to Kelvin about his future plans. She has been encouraging him to stay in school and graduate.

1. Kelvin shyly discusses his schoolwork with you. He has had mainly C's in his major classes, getting A's in physical education and art. He still does not feel comfortable living in Biloxi, and very much enjoys visits to his grandparents' farm. He does not think he can do well in school and wonders why he should return next year. For Kelvin, attending a community or four-year college seems much too difficult. As you listen to Kelvin, you think of this concept from social cognitive career theory.

   a.   associative learning
   b.   instrumental learning
   c.   goal setting
   d.   self-efficacy

2. When talking to you, Kelvin asks, "What will happen if I stay in school next year?" He is starting to find an answer to this question. According to social cognitive career theory, he is raising questions about what concept?

   a.   goals
   b.   outcome expectations
   c.   planned happenstance
   d.   self-efficacy

3. When you ask him what he plans to do if he does not stay in school next year, he says "I will probably keep working at the grocery store." You are asking about which concept of social cognitive career theory?

   a.   barriers
   b.   goals
   c.   outcome expectations
   d.   self-efficacy

4. At times, Kelvin talks to you about what it was like living on a farm in central Mississippi when he was a child. As much as he enjoyed it, he realizes that it did not help him learn more about possibilities that could be open to him now. This discussion refers to what concept of social cognitive career theory?

   a.   background contextual factors
   b.   contextual influences proximal to choice behavior
   c.   goals
   d.   outcome expectations

5. Kelvin tells you that the produce supervisor at the supermarket where he works has appreciated Kelvin's reliability and his hard work. As a result, he has given Kelvin more responsible tasks to complete. The supervisor's actions refer to this concept from social cognitive career theory.

   a.   background contextual factors
   b.   contextual influences proximal to choice behavior
   c.   goals
   d.   outcome expectations

6. Kelvin's mother dropped out of high school in tenth grade. She does not see higher education as a possibility for Kelvin, partly because the family barely has enough money to meet day-to-day expenses. Kelvin's mother's attitude, according to social cognitive career theory, can be considered a (an)

    a.   background contextual factor.
    b.   contextual influence proximal to choice behavior.
    c.   goal.
    d.   outcome expectation.

7. Kelvin's mother's view of possibilities for Kelvin serves, according to social cognitive career theory, as a (an) _____ for Kelvin's career choice.

    a.   barrier
    b.   goal
    c.   outcome expectation
    d.   support

8. Kelvin's older brother is working at a fishery and does not like it. He is thinking about saving money and going to a local community college. He encourages Kelvin to stay in high school and to go to the community college. Kelvin's brother's attitude, according to social cognitive career theory, can be considered a (an)

    a.   barrier.
    b.   goal.
    c.   outcome expectation.
    d.   support.

9. As Kelvin's counselor, you are hopeful that if Kelvin raises his sense of self-efficacy that will positively affect his

    a.   choice actions.
    b.   choice goals.
    c.   interests.
    d.   all of these

10. As Kelvin's counselor you bring up a topic that he has not raised. In Mississippi, it would be expected for some African Americans and Caucasians not to have high expectations of what types of careers African Americans can enter. This could have an impact on Kelvin's choices. According to social cognitive career theory, you are referring to this concept.

    a.   background contextual factors
    b.   contextual influences proximal to choice behavior
    c.   goals
    d.   self efficacy

11. You raise the issue of social biases and discrimination with Kelvin because social cognitive career theory considers this to be a

    a.   major focus of the theory.
    b.   generalization about the world.
    c.   self-observation generalizations about his values.
    d.   task approach skill.

12. You also bring up the confidence that Kelvin's teacher and supervisor at work have in his abilities. You are emphasizing a concept that is made specific by social cognitive career theory.

    a.   barriers
    b.   reinforcement
    c.   role models
    d.   support

13. As Kelvin tries to decide whether or not to continue in high school, you pay particular attention to this social cognitive career theory concept in trying to help him.

    a.   background contextual factors
    b.   his abilities
    c.   his sense of self-efficacy
    d.   his values

APPLYING SOCIAL COGNITIVE CAREER THEORY TO MEN, WOMEN, AND CULTURALLY DIVERSE GROUPS

Does social cognitive career theory have different implications for the career development of men and women? Explain.

_____

_____

_____

_____

What implications does social cognitive career theory have for career counseling with individuals from diverse populations?

_____

_____

_____

_____

STRENGTHS AND LIMITATIONS

What do you see as the strengths and limitations of the application of social cognitive career theory to career counseling?

Strengths   Limitations

_____   _____

_____   _____

_____   _____

_____   _____

_____   _____

KRUMBOLTZ'S SOCIAL LEARNING THEORY: A QUIZ

True or false items: Decide if the following items are more "true" or more "false" as they apply to concepts discussed in this chapter.

T F Q1. A key concept in social cognitive career theory is self-efficacy.

T F Q2. Social cognitive career theory has emphasized reinforcement more than goals.

T F Q3. Outcome expectations refer to what would happen if you do something.

T F Q4. According to social cognitive career theory, goals are self-motivating, which is why individuals can have goals that will take many years to reach.

T F Q5. If you are in graduate school now, your attendance can be called by social cognitive career theory a background contextual factor.

T F Q6. In social cognitive career theory, contextual factors are always barriers to an individual's career development.

T F Q7. Not having enough money to afford to go to graduate school would be called a contextual influence proximal to choice behavior.

T F Q8. In social cognitive career theory, a decisional balance sheet is a counseling method for dealing with barriers.

T F Q9. In social cognitive career theory, planned happenstance is a crucial concept.

T F Q10. In recent years, social cognitive career theory has generated significant research in gender and diversity issues.

Multiple choice items: Select the best answer from the alternatives given. Answer each question from the point of view of social cognitive career theory.

Q11. Like Krumboltz's social learning theory, social cognitive career theory is based on

    a.   the concept of congruence.
    b.   self concept theory.
    c.   trait and factor theory.
    d.   the triadic reciprocal interaction system.

Q12. Which of these concepts do Krumboltz's social learning theory and social cognitive career theory NOT share?

    a.   cognition
    b.   goals
    c.   learning
    d.   self-efficacy

Q13. Jane has varying views of her different abilities. In social cognitive career theory, this statement would refer to which concept?

    a.   capacities
    b.   goals
    c.   outcome expectations
    d.   self-efficacy

Q14. Vicki wants to get a doctorate in clinical psychology. In social cognitive career theory, this statement would refer to which concept?

    a.   context
    b.   goals
    c.   outcome expectations
    d.   self-efficacy

Q15. Chauncey believes that if he practices harder, he will likely become a professional hockey player. In social cognitive career theory, this statement would refer to which concept?

    a.   context
    b.   goals
    c.   outcome expectations
    d.   self-efficacy

Q16. In social cognitive career theory, which of these concepts does NOT lead to performance attainment?

    a.   learning experiences
    b.   outcome expectations
    c.   planned happenstance
    d.   self-efficacy

Q17. In social cognitive career theory, which of these concepts does NOT lead to the development of interests?

    a.   energy
    b.   learning experiences
    c.   outcome expectations
    d.   self-efficacy

Q18. In social cognitive career theory, if you don't have enough money to pay for your medical education, this would be considered

    a.   a barrier.
    b.   a troublesome belief.
    c.   a performance outcome.
    d.   too bad.

Q19. In social cognitive career theory, supports and barriers are most likely to refer to

    a.   background contextual factors.
    b.   contextual influences proximal to choice behavior.
    c.   planned happenstance.
    d.   values about one's self and one's environment.

Q20. In social cognitive career theory, which of these concepts is key to the understanding of the theory?

    a.   balance
    b.   consistency
    c.   constructs
    d.   self-efficacy

Q21. Social cognitive models of career development include a social cognitive model of

    a.   consistency.
    b.   crystallization.
    c.   interests.
    d.   supports.

Q22. A counseling technique that would be most consistent with social cognitive career theory is

    a.   cognitive rehearsal.
    b.   meditation on the ideal career.
    c.   providing support for clients to pursue non-traditional work.
    d.   reflection of feelings.

Q23. A counselor using social cognitive career theory is most likely to attend to

    a.   barriers affecting career choice decisions.
    b.   differentiation of interests.
    c.   search for meaning.
    d.   task approach skills used in career decision-making.

Q24. Social cognitive career theorists are concerned not only about current models of career choice, but have also developed a broader model of

a. crystallization.
b. balance.
c. life satisfaction.
d. planned happenstance.

Q25. Social cognitive career theorists are concerned about occupational negative stereotypes that are attributed to individuals from culturally diverse groups because this may affect the _____ of the individuals.

a. congruence
b. contextual factors
c. persistence
d. self-efficacy

ANSWER KEY

1.	d	11.	a	Q6.	F	Q16.	c
2.	b	12.	d	Q7.	T	Q17.	a
3.	b	13.	c	Q8.	T	Q18.	a
4.	a			Q9.	F	Q19.	b
5.	b			Q10.	T	Q20.	d
6.	b	Q1.	T	Q11.	d	Q21.	c
7.	a	Q2.	F	Q12.	d	Q22.	c
8.	d	Q3.	T	Q13.	d	Q23.	a
9.	d	Q4.	T	Q14.	b	Q24.	c
10.	a	Q5.	F	Q15.	c	Q25.	d

154

CHAPTER 15
CAREER DECISION-MAKING APPROACHES

Descriptive theories

Prescriptive theories

A SPIRITUAL PERSPECTIVE TO CAREER DECION-MAKING

Lifecareer theory (Miller-Tiedeman)

Personal and common realities
Personal reality
Common reality

Spirituality themes
Change
Balance
Energy
Community
Calling
Harmony
Unity

A spiritual approach to career counseling

Let client know their career is their life
Client knows what works and what doesn't
Clients learn to assess experience
Clients set intentions without placing restrictions
Counselors are enthusiastic

A holistic approach to life planning -Hansen

1. Finding work that needs doing in a global context
2. Weaving our lives into a meaningful whole
3. Connecting families and work
4. Valuing pluralism in inclusivity
5. Managing personal transitions and organizational change
6. Exploring spirituality and life purpose

A COGNITIVE INFORMATION PROCESSING APPROACH
Assumptions of the cognitive information processing approach

Self-knowledge

Occupational knowledge

Decision-making skills
Communication
Analysis
Synthesis
Valuing
Execution

The executive processing domain
Self-talk
Self-awareness
Monitoring and control

Materials for counselors and students

Classification of career decision-making styles

Seven-step service delivery system

The role of occupational information
Spirituality
Cognitive information processing approach

The role of assessment instruments
Spirituality
Cognitive information processing approach

Applying the theories to women and culturally diverse populations
Spirituality
Cognitive information processing approach

Counselor issues
Spirituality
Cognitive information processing

CHAPTER 15

CAREER DECISION-MAKING APPROACHES

EXERCISE 15.1

SPIRITUAL AND INTERNAL RESOURCES IN CAREER DEVELOPMENT

E. 1. Why is it important that you make your own career choice rather than have a parent or someone else make it for you?

_____

_____

_____

_____

E. 2. How would you react to a forced career change (such as being laid off)? How would you cope with that change? (Change)

_____

_____

_____

_____

E. 3. Give an example of when you were tired, yet were doing something that you really enjoyed, and felt a burst of energy and plunged into the activity. (Energy)

_____

_____

_____

_____

E. 4. How does the term *calling* apply to your career choice? In what way do you feel called (or not called) to your profession? (Calling)

_____

_____

_____

_____

_____

EXERCISE 15.2

CAREER DECISION-MAKING SKILLS

E. 5. What was it like when you first felt strongly that you needed to think through or rethink a career choice? (Communication)

_____

_____

_____

_____

_____

E. 6. Describe the experience of reexamining your abilities, interests, and values. (Analysis)

_____

_____

_____

_____

_____

E. 7. When you reexamined your abilities, interests, and values what did you do to arrive at one or more choices? (Synthesis)

_____

_____

_____

_____

E. 8. As you considered your choices, how did you evaluate the choices as to how they would affect your life? (Valuing)

_____

_____

_____

_____

E. 9. How did you decide what actions to take in following through on your career choice? What did that feel like? (Execution)

_____

_____

_____

_____

_____

COUNSELING JASON USING BLOCH AND RICHMOND'S APPROACH TO SPIRITUALITY AND MILLER-TIEDEMAN'S LIFECAREER THEORY

Having been an insurance salesperson for 26 years, Jason is questioning whether or not he wants to continue doing this. At age 52, he is married with a son who is a senior in college and a daughter in dental school. His wife is a marketing manager. For over 20 years, Jason has been involved in working with his church, serving as a Sunday school teacher and as a member of the church's executive board. He is growing weary of selling insurance. In past years, he believed that he was being helpful to his customers by providing insurance for their families in case of a death in the family. This rationale no longer satisfies him. He feels that he wants to help others more than he is doing now. He is considering changing fields to the ministry or social work.

Use the spiritual concepts of Bloch and Richmond to conceptualize Jason's worries. Also, apply Miller-Tiedeman's approach to helping him decide on which new career path to consider, if any.

1. Jason talks to you about a recent experience he has found meaningful. After church one day, he was approached by a woman who was concerned that her husband had lost a job and was now despondent. He was able to help her get support for her husband and also financial support for her family. After this incident, he felt better than he had a long time. He felt a new sense of purpose and sense of being. According to Bloch and Richmond, he was experiencing _____ in his life.

   a. balance
   b. calling
   c. energy
   d. testing out

2. Jason has felt differently about his church in the last few years. Rather than just teaching Sunday school and attending services, he has felt a much greater sense of belonging to this group than he has before. He very much appreciates the experience of this feeling. According to Bloch and Richmond, he is experiencing a sense of _____ in his life.

   a. balance
   b. community
   c. energy
   d. internalization

3. When Jason talks to you about possibly leaving his insurance sales job, he is concerned about where his future will lead. You are aware of the anxiety that Jason is experiencing as he talks with you about this. According to Bloch and Richmond, he is experiencing _____ in his life.

   a. balance
   b. change
   c. energy
   d. unity

4. Jason describes the routine that he experiences in his sales work. He no longer has the energy for it that he did before. According to Bloch and Richmond, he wants to have a sense of _____ in his life.

   a. calling
   b. harmony
   c. rebirth
   d. internalization

5. Using Miller-Tiedeman's Lifecareer theory, you look at Jason's current concern as

   a. a career decision-making crisis.
   b. a part of an ongoing crisis.
   c. one aspect of his life, which is his career.
   d. reason to seek psychiatric consultation.

6 When Jason asks you what advice you have for him as to his career direction, you use Lifecareer theory as a guide and suggest that he

    a.   become satisfied with his current occupation as an insurance salesperson.
    b.   is the best judge of what to do.
    c.   pursue the ministry.
    d.   wait until he receives a calling from God.

7. When Jason tells you that it was a mistake for him to have stayed in insurance all of these years, you follow Lifecareer theory and suggest to him that he

    a.   counter this troublesome belief.
    b.   does not need to judge his own life.
    c.   is correct, he should have left the insurance industry.
    d.   rewrite his life, stressing the need to develop unity.

8. Jason talks to you about making plans to leave his job in insurance and to enter a seminary to become a minister, you follow Lifecareer theory and are

    a.   countering this troublesome belief.
    b.   enthusiastic about the possibility of his decision to change his life.
    c.   raising issues regarding the pros and cons of this decision.
    d.   reminding him that if he were called to the ministry, he would know this.

IDENTIFYING TERESA'S CAREER DECISION-MAKING SKILLS USING THE COGNITIVE INFORMATION PROCESSING APPROACH

Teresa is a 19-year-old college sophomore who is unsure of her major and unsure what she might do after she graduates. Her parents are both engineers, but she has little interest in science. When she was in elementary school she wanted to be an actor and a model. In middle school, she thought she might like to be in the military or perhaps be a police officer. In high school she became interested in broadcasting and politics. She had worked in a restaurant when she was in high school and could see herself managing a restaurant. Now that she is in college, she looks back at all of her interests and believes that all but being a model or actor are possible for her. She has sought counseling to see if she should pursue one of these areas or possibly one that she has not thought about.

In the following questions, identify the decision-making skill or information processing domain that Teresa is using.

9. Teresa is becoming increasingly uncomfortable with not knowing what she will do upon graduation. This has been made more pronounced by her parents asking her every few weeks what she will do, as well as her knowledge that her college requires her to select a major in three months. According to career cognitive information processing theory, Teresa is in this phase.

    a.   communication
    b.   analysis
    c.   synthesis
    d.   valuation
    e.   execution

160

10. Teresa uses inventories and discussion with her counselor to reexamine her abilities, interests, and values. According to career cognitive information processing theory, Teresa is in this phase.

    a.   communication
    b.   analysis
    c.   synthesis
    d.   valuing
    e.   execution

11. Now that she feels stress to choose a career, Teresa says to herself, "I need to make choosing a major and a career a priority as I need to stop putting the decision off so that I can make plans." According to career cognitive information processing theory, Teresa is thinking about decision-making through

    a.   communication.
    b.   analysis.
    c.   synthesis.
    d.   self-talk.

12. Teresa is starting to think about several communications and business management occupations. She makes a fairly long list of occupations that she will start to choose from. According to career cognitive information processing theory, Teresa is in this phase.

    a.   analysis
    b.   synthesis
    c.   self-monitoring
    d.   valuing

13. Now Teresa is in a position where she can evaluate her choices. She starts to put broadcast journalism near the top of the list, with store management second. According to career cognitive information processing theory, Teresa is in this phase.

    a.   synthesis
    b.   monitoring and control
    c.   valuing
    d.   execution

14. Teresa is aware that she is valuing her options. She is feeling pleased that she is able to understand that she is making progress in her career decision-making. She believes that she has been able to broaden her options, and then narrow them down in a helpful and organized way. According to career cognitive information processing theory, Teresa is thinking about decision-making through

    a.   synthesis.
    b.   monitoring and control.
    c.   valuing.
    d.   execution.

15. Considering broadcast journalism and retail management to be her two top priorities, Teresa decides to do some new activities. She has an interview at the university radio station so that she can volunteer as a disc jockey. She also is arranging for a summer job in a retail store owned by a friend of her uncle's. The owner knows she has an interest in retailing and is willing to not only have her work for him but also show her some management aspects of retailing. According to career cognitive information processing theory, Teresa is in this phase.

    a.   synthesis
    b.   monitoring and control
    c.   valuing
    d.   execution

APPLYING A SPIRITUAL APPROACH TO CAREER DEVELOPMENT TO MEN, WOMEN, AND CULTURALLY DIVERSE GROUPS

Do spiritual approaches to career development have different implications for the career development of men and women? Explain.

_____

_____

_____

_____

_____

_____

_____

What implications do spiritual approaches to career development have for career counseling with individuals from diverse populations?

_____

_____

_____

_____

_____

_____

_____

APPLYING A COGNITIVE INFORMATION PROCESSING APPROACH TO MEN, WOMEN, AND CULTURALLY DIVERSE GROUPS

Does a cognitive information processing approach to career development have different implications for the career development of men and women? Explain.

_____

_____

_____

_____

_____

_____

What implications does a cognitive information processing approach have for career counseling with individuals from diverse populations?

_____

_____

_____

_____

_____

_____

STRENGTHS AND LIMITATIONS

What do you see as the strengths and limitations of the application of spiritual approaches to career development to career counseling?

Strengths	Limitations
_____	_____
_____	_____
_____	_____
_____	_____

STRENGTHS AND LIMITATIONS

What do you see as the strengths and limitations of the application of a cognitive information processing approach to career counseling?

Strengths   Limitations

_____   _____

_____   _____

_____   _____

_____   _____

_____   _____

CAREER DECISION-MAKING THEORIES: A QUIZ

True or false items: Decide if the following items are more "true" or more "false" as they apply to concepts discussed in this chapter.

T   F   Q1.   A descriptive career decision-making method is one which suggests that there is a best way to choose a career.

T   F   Q2.   Knowing what would be a good career for your child is an example of the concept of common reality.

T   F   Q3.   In Bloch and Richmond's spiritual approach to career development, individuals seek out balance among many roles in their lives, not just in their work life.

T   F   Q4.   According to Lifecareer theory, one should recognize that there are natural forces that restrain the flow of one's career and one should fight against them.

T   F   Q5.   According to Lifecareer theory, clients should set intentions and not put time restrictions on them; rather clients can follow or track their intentions.

T   F   Q6.   A cognitive information processing approach to career development takes both affective and cognitive aspects of career decision-making into consideration.

T   F   Q7.   Becoming aware of how one's thoughts affect one's career decision-making is a significant aspect of a cognitive information processing approach to career development.

T   F   Q8.   In the cognitive information processing approach to career development, networking is one of the five major decision-making skills.

T   F   Q9.   In the cognitive information processing approach to career development, the knowledge domains of self and occupation are similar to the first two steps of trait and factor theory.

T   F   Q10. The cognitive information processing approach to career development is similar in its philosophy to a spiritual approach to career development.

164

Multiple choice items: Select the best answer from the alternatives given. Answer each question from the point of view of career decision-making approaches.

Q11.   Which of the following theories follows a prescriptive approach to career decision-making?

    a.   Bloch and Richmond's spirituality theory
    b.   cognitive processing approach
    c.   Hansen's holistic approach to life planning
    d.   Miller-Tiedeman's Lifecareer theory

Q12.   According to Bloch and Richmond's spirituality theory, when change in someone's career occurs by chance rather than through connected events, it is called

    a.   balance.
    b.   lifecareer.
    c.   planned happenstance.
    d.   synchronicity.

Q13.   According to Bloch and Richmond's spirituality theory, finding joy in one's work is an indication that a person has found a

    a.   calling.
    b.   job.
    c.   meaningful transition.
    d.   network.

Q14.   According to Bloch and Richmond's spirituality theory, all but one of these is an element of spirituality in career counseling.

    a.   balance
    b.   curiosity
    c.   energy
    d.   unity

Q15.   According to Lifecareer theory, which of these would be an example of an appropriate approach to career counseling?

    a.   choosing one career plan and following it
    b.   choosing three or four plans that can be modified
    c.   focusing on one's meta-cognitions
    d.   focusing on task approach skills

Q16.   According to Lifecareer theory, passing judgment on the client's reality should only be done by

    a.   the client.
    b.   the client's parents or spouse.
    c.   the counselor.
    d.   no one.

Q17. Hansen's holistic approach to life planning is most similar to that of

    a.   Bloch and Richmond's spirituality approach.
    b.   cognitive information processing.
    c.   Krumboltz's social learning approach.
    d.   Myers-Briggs type theory.

Q18. An important aspect of Hansen's holistic approach to life planning is

    a.   cognitive rehearsal.
    b.   examining a connection between family and work.
    c.   looking at the plot and setting of the client's story.
    d.   reinforcing client's increased feelings of self-efficacy.

Q19. Which of the following is NOT a major processing domain according to the cognitive information processing approach to career development?

    a.   executive
    b.   decision-making
    c.   knowledge
    d.   prescriptive

Q20. Elaborating on ideas that are related to career choice or crystallizing them is associated with which phase of the cognitive information processing approach to career development?

    a.   communication
    b.   analysis
    c.   synthesis
    d.   valuing
    e.   execution

Q21. When one starts to know that there is a career issue that needs to be addressed, the individual is likely to be in this phase of the cognitive information processing approach to career development.

    a.   communication
    b.   analysis
    c.   synthesis
    d.   valuing
    e.   execution

Q22. Evaluating the career choices that an individual has synthesized is likely to be found in this phase of the cognitive information processing approach to career development.

    a.   communication
    b.   analysis
    c.   synthesis
    d.   valuing
    e.   execution

Q23. Writing a resume, having interviews for jobs, and doing volunteer work are activities likely to be found in this phase of the cognitive information processing approach to career development.

    a.   communication
    b.   analysis
    c.   synthesis
    d.   valuing
    e.   execution

Q24. Alfred made notes of how he went through the CASVE cycle. By doing so, he was in this phase or process of the executive domain of the cognitive information processing approach to career development.

    a.   communication
    b.   monitoring and self control
    c.   self-awareness
    d.   self-talk

Q25. Which of these approaches is most concerned with changing social and economic factors occurring throughout the world?

    a.   Bloch and Richmond's spiritual approach
    b.   cognitive information processing
    c.   Hansen's holistic approach to life planning
    d.   Miller-Tiedeman's Lifecareer theory

ANSWER KEY

1.	c	11.	d	Q6.	T	Q16.	d
2.	b	12.	b	Q7.	T	Q17.	a
3.	b	13.	c	Q8.	F	Q18.	b
4.	b	14.	b	Q9.	T	Q19.	d
5.	c	15.	d	Q10.	F	Q20.	c
6.	b	Q1.	F	Q11.	b	Q21.	a
7.	b	Q2.	T	Q12.	d	Q22.	d
8.	b	Q3.	T	Q13.	a	Q23.	e
9.	a	Q4.	F	Q14.	b	Q24.	b
10.	b	Q5.	T	Q15.	b	Q25.	c

CHAPTER 16
THEORIES IN COMBINATION

An outline of career development theories

Lapan and Turner's contextually responsive career counseling system for young people

Combining life-span theory with trait and factor and career decision-making theories

Childhood

Adolescence

Late adolescence and adulthood

Adult career development

Combining trait and factor theories

Combining career decision-making theories

The counselor's choice — your choice

Noncounseling applications of theories

Screening methods

Paper-and-pencil methods

Computerized guidance systems

Internet

Assessment inventories

Career information

Ethical issues

Special counseling issues

Group career counseling

Career counseling as a related issue

Changing work settings

Placement counseling

Use of assessment instruments in theories

Occupational classification systems and career development theories

How theories apply to career development issues of women

How theories apply to cultural diversity issues in career development

Counselor issues

Trait and factor theories

Life-span theories

Career decision-making theories

Sociological and economic approaches

168

CHAPTER 16

THEORIES IN COMBINATION

EXERCISE 16.1

SUMMARY OF EXERCISES

E. 1. Review the exercises in each of the previous chapters of this manual. List three of the ones that you would most likely use with a small group of clients that you might work with. Describe why you would use these exercises and how they relate to the theory that the exercise is based on. (If you are interested in working with young children, consider using the activities that are mentioned in Chapter 7.)

A. Exercise from Chapter ___

_____

_____

_____

_____

B. Exercise from Chapter ___

_____

_____

_____

_____

C. Exercise from Chapter___

_____

_____

_____

_____

_____

QUESTIONS ABOUT CHAPTER 16

1. Which of the following is NOT a trait and factor theory?

   a. Holland's theory
   b. Phillips's theory
   c. Myers-Briggs type theory
   d. work adjustment theory

2. Which of these theories is most likely to be used with children?

   a. Gottfredson's
   b. narrative
   c. Phillips's
   d. work adjustment theory

3. Career maturity is a concept that pertains most directly to

   a. adolescents.
   b. adults.
   c. children.
   d. retired people.

4. The purpose of using career inventories to screen clients is to help decide who

   a. is a security risk.
   b. can benefit from career counseling.
   c. needs outplacement counseling.
   d. can use the Internet without being monitored.

5. The DISCOVER computer system follows this theory most closely.

   a. Gottfredson's
   b. family therapy
   c. constructivist
   d. trait and factor

6. The Internet provides all but one of the following types of career-related information.

   a. assessment instruments
   b. names of career counseling organizations
   c. job postings
   d. all of these are available on the Internet

7. Which of the following theories can be applied to group career counseling?

   a. cognitive information processing theory
   b. spiritual theories
   c. narrative career counseling
   d. all of these

170

8. The "job club" approach developed by Azrin and Besalel for outplacement counseling is based on
_____ principles.

    a.   behavioral
    b.   cognitive
    c.   ethical
    d.   narrative

9. When using assessment instruments in career counseling,

    a.   most theories suggest appropriate instruments to be used.
    b.   any instrument can be used for any theory.
    c.   no assessment information should be used; only occupational information should be used.
    d.   tests should be used but not inventories.

10. Classification systems have been developed

    a.   separately for each career development theory.
    b.   to categorize occupations.
    c.   to categorize theories.
    d.   to reward occupational information-seeking.

11. Comparing one's own life stage experience to that of the client might fit with this theory.

    a.   Myers-Briggs type theory
    b.   narrative theory
    c.   Phillips's theory
    d.   Super's developmental theory

12. Pointing out inequalities in the labor market that negatively affect minorities would fit this class of
theories.

    a.   career decision-making
    b.   life-span
    c.   sociological
    d.   trait and factor

A REVIEW OF ALL THEORIES DESCRIBED IN THE TEXT: A QUIZ

True or false items: Decide if the following items are more "true" or more "false" as they apply to
concepts discussed in the textbook.

T F Q1. Trait and factor theory can be applied to the entire life-span.

T F Q2. The essential element of trait and factor theory is that of giving the client occupational
information.

T F Q3. Work adjustment theory is primarily concerned with the measurement of abilities and
values rather than interests.

T F Q4. Holland views his types as a way of viewing personality rather than abilities.

T F Q5. Myers-Briggs type theory assesses interests, abilities, values, and personality.

T F Q6. An important aspect of Gottfredson's theory is understanding how social influences might influence individuals' career choices.

T F Q7. Holland would advocate that adolescents assess their career maturity before taking the Self-Directed Search.

T F Q8. According to Hopson and Adams, the most likely initial reaction to being fired is to be immobilized and shocked.

T F Q9. Susan Phillips and her colleagues study the ways that clients tell their stories or describe their career life histories.

T F Q10. Human capital theory is concerned with the investment in time and money that individuals plan to make as they go about choosing a career.

Multiple choice items: Select the best answer from the alternatives given.

Q11. Congruence is a concept that is associated with this theory.

    a.   Holland's
    b.   Miller-Tiedeman's
    c.   Phillips's
    d.   trait and factor

Q12. Being in one's inner world rather than the outside world is a concept associated with

    a.   Gottfredson's theory.
    b.   human capital theory.
    c.   Myers-Briggs type theory.
    d.   work adjustment theory.

Q13. Which of the following theories examines the effect of all types of relationships on individuals' career development?

    a.   attachment theory
    b.   family therapy theories
    c.   Phillips's theory
    d.   Roe's theory

Q14. Which of these stages in Super's life-span theory is an adult most like to go through first?

    a.   disengagement
    b.   establishment
    c.   exploration
    d.   maintenance

Q15.   Testing out is a concept associated with which one of these theories?

    a.   Gottfredson's
    b.   Hopson and Adams's
    c.   Miller-Tiedeman's
    d.   trait and factor

Q16.   The concept of recycling is associated with which one of these career development theories?

    a.   ecological
    b.   Gottfredson's
    c.   Myers-Briggs type theory
    d.   Super's

Q17.   Attention to the actions of others is a concern of this theory.

    a.   Roe's
    b.   Gottfredson's
    c.   Phillips's
    d.   work adjustment

Q18.   Which of the following is a concept found in Holland's theory?

    a.   differentiation
    b.   executive processing domain
    c.   maintenance
    d.   self-directedness

Q19.   In cognitive information processing theory, which of the following is NOT a generic information processing skill?

    a.   communication
    b.   consistency
    c.   execution
    d.   synthesis

Q20.   Which of these theories helps most in understanding the career development of children?

    a.   cognitive information processing theory
    b.   Gottfredson's theory
    c.   narrative career theory
    d.   trait and factor theory

Q21.   Planned happenstance is a concept important to

    a.   attachment theory.
    b.   constructivist theory.
    c.   Krumboltz's social learning theory.
    d.   social cognitive career theory.

Q22. Which of the following concepts is NOT important in social cognitive theory?

    a.   barriers
    b.   goals
    c.   observational learning
    d.   self-efficacy

Q23. Prestige is a concept that is important in Gottfredson's theory and

    a.   Holland's theory.
    b.   human capital theory.
    c.   Hopson and Adams crisis theory.
    d.   status attainment theory.

Q24. Which of the following has the most complex explanation of how individuals choose careers?

    a.   Holland's theory
    b.   Marcia's theory
    c.   social cognitive career theory
    d.   trait and factor theory

Q25. "Balance" and "calling" are concepts associated with

    a.   cognitive information processing theory.
    b.   Gottfredson's theory.
    c.   spirituality career development theory.
    d.   Hopson and Adams's crisis theory.

ANSWER KEY

1.	b	11.	d	Q7.	F	Q17.	c
2.	a	12.	c	Q8.	T	Q18.	a
3.	a			Q9.	F	Q19.	b
4.	b	Q1.	F	Q10.	T	Q20.	b
5.	d	Q2.	F	Q11.	a	Q21.	c
6.	d	Q3.	T	Q12.	c	Q22.	c
7.	d	Q4.	T	Q13.	c	Q23.	d
8.	a	Q5.	F	Q14.	c	Q24.	c
9.	a	Q6.	T	Q15.	b	Q25.	c
10.	b			Q16.	d